Strategic Church

Embracing a wider vision

Hugh Osgood

malcolm down
PUBLISHING

Copyright © Hugh Osgood 2025
First published 2025 by Malcolm Down Publishing Ltd
www.malcolmdown.co.uk

28 27 26 25   6 5 4 3 2 1

The right of Hugh Osgood to be identified as the author of this work has been asserted by him in accordance with the Copyright, Designs and Patents Act 1988.

All rights reserved. No part of this publication may be reproduced, stored in a retrieval system, or transmitted in any other form or by any means, electronic, mechanical, photocopying, recording or otherwise, without the prior permission of the publisher.

British Library Cataloguing in Publication Data
A catalogue record for this book is available from the British Library.

ISBN 978-1-917455-16-9

Unless otherwise marked, Scripture quotations are taken from the Holy Bible, New International Version (Anglicised edition). Copyright © 1979, 1984, 2011 Biblica. Used by permission of Hodder & Stoughton Ltd, an Hachette UK company. All rights reserved.

'NIV' is a registered trademark of Biblica.
UK trademark number 1448790.

Scripture quotations marked 'ESV' are taken from the Holy Bible, English Standard Version (Anglicised). Published by HarperCollins Publishers © 2001 Crossway Bibles, a publishing ministry of Good News Publishers. Used by permission. All rights reserved.

Scripture quotations marked 'KJV' are from The Authorised (King James) Version. Rights in the Authorised Version in the United Kingdom are vested in the Crown. Reproduced by permission of the Crown's patentee, Cambridge University Press.

Cover design by Angela Selfe
London borough map: https://d-maps.com/carte.php?num_car=289235&lang=en

Art direction by Sarah Grace

Printed in the UK

Acknowledgements

This is the second book in a series. Once again I'll be using personal stories alongside biblical accounts to illustrate lessons about life and leadership. I'm grateful to Paul Syrstad, my one-time fellow podcaster, who, having drawn personal stories from me offline, somehow managed to persuade me to . . . 'now just tell everybody'. As I look back, I cannot say a big enough thank you to my wife, Marion, for being with me every step of the way.

Contents

Foreword	7
Introduction	11
1. Positioning: *The wind and the tent*	19
2. Waiting: *Finding a focus*	29
3. Assessing: *Pictures of hope*	41
4. Sharing: *Gaining a hearing*	51
5. Launching: *The blaze and the blast*	63
6. Expanding: *Broadening the appeal*	73
7. Partnering: *Finding fellow travellers*	81
8. Engaging: *Walking together*	91
9. Persisting: *Pursuing with passion*	99
10. Coordinating: *Staying on track*	109
11. Branding: *Living with labels*	119
12. Buffeting: *Cultural cross-currents*	127
13. Re-envisioning: *Recasting the net*	135
14. Maturing: *A necessary step forward*	145
Postscript: *Strategic possibilities*	155

Foreword

The strategic importance of cities in the plans and purposes of God cannot be over-estimated. From Suza to Jerusalem and from Jerusalem to Rome, the scriptural narrative overflows with cities. Paul's major letters were written to cities that he had visited on his missionary journeys, and the book of Acts plots the propagation of the gospel in terms of a city-to-city shift beginning in Jerusalem and ending in Rome. Luke's purpose seems clear to me – the story of the spread of the Church is from the city which is the centre of the Jewish world to the city that is the centre of the political world. Cities still matter in the plans and purposes of God. We will not reach the world without reaching our cities. That is why Hugh Osgood's work is of such strategic importance. He understands the plans and purposes of God for cities and is able to articulate it in a way that makes such sense. This book, alongside the others in this series, is very important.

I have known Hugh for almost thirty years. Our paths first crossed when I was working for the Evangelical Alliance. I led their work in the UK around church engagement, mission, evangelism and prayer. I was working with over 3,500 churches at the time, a large number of which were in London. Hugh was a key voice in the church in the UK capital, as he is now. His tireless call for gospel collaboration across churches, cultures and generations was a trumpet sound of gospel hope. He knew, intuitively, theologically and pragmatically, that London needed a Church that was united. His disdain for fractured relationships, empire builders and silos has always been a fundamental part of his message, and his life. Long before most others were talking about it, Hugh was prophesying of a London Church that would be enriched, enabled and beautified by cultural, ethnic and theological diversity. He was celebrating its potential before almost anyone else I know. He saw that God was raising up this rich blend of backgrounds and beliefs for the betterment of gospel mission. As a consequence, he has spent decades calling for more intentional sharing of resources, strategy and planning. He has not given up on this ideal. And I am glad that he has stuck at it.

Jump forward to today, and I have returned to London to lead Kensington Temple London City Church. Hugh speaks of it in this volume with kindness. His words spring from the posture that my predecessor, Colin Dye, took towards London's gospel unity. I honour Colin for that stance, as Hugh does here. Our church is large, diverse and multi-sited. We have 126 nationalities represented at the time of my writing, thousands of members, almost 600 cells or small groups, and over thirty congregations across the city. We also link to a number of cities and nations around the world. As I read Hugh's apposite insights into what the Church in London needs to think about and do now to be effective, I found myself scribbling notes and kneeling in prayer. There are vital lessons to learn still. Shared prayer, shared resources, spiritual mapping, shared and individual responsibility and depth of relationships are all mentioned in one way or another in this book, and they all matter.

Speaking of two other great cities, Dickens once wrote, 'It was the best of times, and it was the worst of times.' This could be said of the scene in London today too. We are in the foothills of remarkable days but the call for unity and collaboration is still crucial. Having been back in the capital for seven months now, after almost a decade of absence, I find myself yearning for a city-wide strategy

Foreword

of prayer, gospel partnership and deep relationships. No church, no matter how large, can do it alone. God's design is that none of us have got every ingredient of his recipe. He has created us to be interdependent. And what is true of churches is also true of leaders. That is why Hugh's work matters so much. He is still beating the same drum, still calling for better thinking, better sharing and better collaboration. He was right thirty years ago, and he is right today.

As you read his words, I pray that something will spark in your spirit. I believe that God is not only calling London churches to this vision, but that he is also calling city-to-city networks into existence. May God use Hugh's voice to help this to happen.

Malcolm Duncan
Senior Minister and Apostolic Leader of KTLCC
London, February 2025

Introduction

A group of university students persuaded me to take a week off from the comfort of my young family and join them on a summer break in a primitive Welsh cottage in the middle of nowhere. They'd grown to know me in the context of their college Christian Union and thought it would be fun to have me around with them more informally. They were an adventurous bunch and decided to climb Yr Wyddfa (Snowdon) using the Crib Goch route. This was fine by me as I'd climbed in the Lake District at the end of my first year at university. But on one particular ledge, with a steep section to climb ahead of us, a member of our party had had enough. We tried persuading him to keep going by stressing that others had passed this way before, but he pointed to a pile of cigarette ends on the track and said, 'And how nervous must they have been?' In a sentence he thought he'd summed up his own difficulty, but nerves were only part of his problem. Unlike the rest of us he'd come on the climb because he'd felt obliged, and right at this moment feeling obliged wasn't giving him a strong enough sense of purpose to keep going. We tried describing the view from the peak and the sense of achievement he'd feel on arrival, but nothing worked. In the end we resorted to Macbeth's fatalism, '[If] returning were as tedious as go o'er' and on that basis we pressed forward.[1]

The panic experienced by that student on the ledge halfway up Crib Goch reminds me that there's always a risk of becoming stuck

---

1. Shakespeare, *Macbeth*, Act 3, Scene 4.

if we fail to see the significance of what we've taken on. Just coming along out of a sense of obligation, or pressing on because it's equally hard to go back, will rarely be enough. This book is about giving us all a stronger sense of purpose by reminding us that we each have a part to play in God's strategic plan. The nature of that role will vary, but one thing is certain: once we've caught sight of the greatness of that plan we'll never again question the significance of our contribution, no matter how great or small it might seem. It's having that sense of purpose that will make sure we never get stuck.

God's plan for his Church unfolds at multiple levels. God is a strategist and he is constantly shaping and reshaping his Church so it can impact every nation, in every generation and at every level of society. He wants his Church to be multigenerational, multi-ethnic and socio-economically diverse. He also wants it to be authentic, relevant, relational and inspirational, which it will be once every member has grasped the significance of what God is doing and becomes excited about communicating it.

We may find ourselves playing out our personal role locally, regionally, nationally or internationally, and that role might see us inspiring thousands or impacting just one or two. In this book there will be times when I'll be talking about inspiring hundreds, and occasionally thousands, but those among us who can do that only succeed because they know how to inspire the ones and twos. A crowd, no matter how large, is inspired individually, and while it's being inspired it needs those who can keep the inspiration going at a personal level. It's not hard to see that the more inspiration there is in an environment, the easier it is for everyone to keep on inspiring each other. This might not be exactly true of the environment you're in right now, but hopefully by the end of this book it will be true of the renewed environment you'll have begun helping to create.

Introduction

Now with so much talk of inspiration you may ask, 'Why isn't this book called *Inspirational Church*?' Well it could be, but I believe that for anyone to be inspirational they'll have to have grasped the significance of the vision they want to share – and I'm definitely seeking to produce vision-sharers and not just vision-holders. I'm aware that the vision you might be working on while reading this book could be about almost anything. But I have to admit that, although a lot of what I share should help any visionary to think strategically, I'm actually directing my comments primarily towards those seeking to reshape churches or initiate church-related projects. Right now there is a fantastic creative longing that pulsates within the Church as people yearn to express what God is stirring in their hearts and minds. This is particularly true among twenty- and thirty-year-olds, and the personal experiences I relate in this book are drawn from a time when I was only a decade further on in my life's journey. Even so, the principles I'm sharing can be grasped and applied at any age. They're basically a set of key steps to thinking and acting in a strategic way, but they will involve some openness to innovation, so it's worth slipping in a request at this point for flexible thinking.

Recently I was asked to engage with younger leaders to find out how willing they and their peers would be to take over some of the UK's long-established Christian societies. To have summed up their reply as 'not keen at all' would have been an understatement, and I totally sympathised. These societies were birthed by start-up generations in the past, so why can't a new start-up generation produce something that meets today's needs more relevantly? I know it's radical to think this way, but if we allow it to happen, the fresh energy would almost certainly attract others and galvanise them into action. In reality, no one needs permission to rethink a situation but sometimes provocation to rethink can be useful.

So gentle provocation is my aim. As I write, I have a few specific friends in mind: some are in their thirties reshaping churches; others are launching projects and planting churches in their twenties. Of course, I have friends who are older, and many of them have the same quality as those who are younger – tremendous potential that needs to be encouraged. My aim is that no one will miss out. The apostle Paul may have been in his thirties and forties but Moses was a strategic thinker in his eighties. And if you have doubts about being labelled as a person with potential, I believe you're about to be surprised. If you see the significance of what God is doing, even a little potential can go a very long way, especially when placed alongside the potential of others who are willing to be fellow vision-sharers and join you in a strategic initiative.

As this book is the second of a series, I need to explain how the series works. In part I'm seeking to share lessons from my past. This time they relate to those years when, having previously seen God raise up a community-focused church, I found God repositioning me to share a vision that ended up seeing that church reconfigured. Although I try to keep details and dates to a minimum so as not to freeze things in the past, this time there'll be a few unavoidable time pointers, which I trust won't reduce the continuing relevance of the lessons that can be learnt.

Those of you who know me well wouldn't expect me to present my personal journey without seeking to line up the steps I took with those we can see in Scripture. During this period it was primarily Paul's time at Ephesus that I kept in focus.[2] I'll be using the fourteen

---

2. Acts 18:19-21; 19:1 – 20:1.

Introduction

steps that I identified in Paul's journey and could also trace in mine as I take you through the book. They are: positioning, waiting, assessing, sharing, launching, expanding, partnering, engaging, persisting, coordinating, branding, buffeting, re-envisioning and maturing. The fourteenth actually seemed to apply more to me than to Paul, Paul having clearly matured much more speedily than I did.

Obviously I accept that both Paul's journey and mine will seem very different from the path that may be lying ahead for you. Many of you will be in churches where there's already a well-established strategic purpose. This may be summed up as 'We are a worshipping community bringing life and hope to the locality by sharing God's word, and providing care'. There will also be some of you who are engaged in projects that have an equally well-established strategic purpose. In the end, being strategic has nothing to do with how well-established or new our purpose is, or how simple or complex it may be. In reality, a purpose that can be expressed simply is more likely to be taken up effectively than one that is difficult to remember or hard to explain. What is truly exciting is having everyone who is involved in a church or project embracing its strategic purpose with an enthusiasm that shows a confident belief that God has raised up that church or project to successfully fulfil its vision. When you see a church or project in that way, you'll know that there is little likelihood of anyone getting stuck halfway up the mountain you're about to climb.

Now all that I've said above could be dismissed as 'easier said than done', but ironically it's confidence in being strategic that can actually increase a church or project's strategic impact. Read on and I'll try to prove this to you while I share with you Paul's story from Ephesus and mine from south-east London. I'd only ask you to bear in mind that while my telling of Paul's story can be checked against

Scripture, some who have journeyed with me may wish to tell my story differently. I have sought to be open and honest, however, and am happy for you to learn from my failings.

Six principles to keep in mind while reading this book

1. God is a strategist.
2. God is constantly shaping his Church to ensure it can input relevantly into every level of society.
3. God wants his Church to be multigenerational, multi-ethnic and socio-economically diverse.
4. God wants every church member to see the wider significance of their local church, or church-based initiative.
5. God will, from time to time, raise up fresh expressions of church that he expects the Church to welcome and support.
6. In order to create such expressions, God will inspire vision-sharers whose breadth of understanding and depth of humility should make them effective mobilisers and caring influencers.

Preparing

Positioning — Waiting — Assessing — Sharing — Launching

1. Positioning: *The wind and the tent*

For three years the Twelve have been gathered in a close-knit group around Jesus, and somehow he's always been the one to manage the multitudes. Now, as they look out across an open square at 9 o'clock on a Jerusalem morning, handling the wind-gathered crowd is their responsibility. Questions and comments fill the air as festival attendees from far and wide try to make sense of the multilingual explosion of joy they've just witnessed. The Twelve never expected it to happen like this, but the wind that's drawn the crowd also filled the upper room where, just a few moments ago, they and a hundred others were praying. It was the wind of God's Spirit. As the Holy Spirit flooded their lives they were transformed in an instant. They'd spilled out onto the square and couldn't help but express their heartfelt praise to God, albeit in languages they'd never learnt. But strangely the visitors in the crowd understood them plainly enough, and now there's a lot of explaining to do.[3] Can the crowd grasp that the words of praise, amazement and thankfulness they've just heard in their own languages actually prove that God is now doing something he's planned way back before creation?

As we think about God's ability to position us, it's really good to start by focusing on the Twelve as they pick up their new responsibility. They've just been empowered by the Holy Spirit at Pentecost and are having to work through the practical consequences. This will always be the case, for us as it was for them. Putting it as simply as possible,

---

3. Acts 2:1-41.

if we're to see our churches and ministries achieve specific goals for God, we'll need to be people who are not only willing to be caught up by the wind of God's Spirit but are able to commit to working with the Holy Spirit as we see the practical unfolding of God's plan.

Now there's probably nothing that can bring us down to earth more quickly than turning from the book of Acts to my personal story. My recruitment for a particular strategic assignment (the kind of assignment this book is about) also involved a wind. Nine areas of London were holding evangelistic campaigns ahead of a major, single-location, capital-wide event booked for the following year. In south-east London the church I was leading was preparing to be fully engaged as soon as the 3,000-seater tent was pitched on Blackheath. Once the tent was up and the appointed evangelists headed our way, all the counsellor training, leafleting and inviting we and others had been involved in began to prove worthwhile. Night after night the tent was packed, and on the final Saturday morning I was in charge, hosting a children's programme. As the young participants cheered and clapped their way through the quizzes, games and stage presentations, I could hear the sound of flapping canvas.

As the wind increased, the excitement of the children also rose. They seemed unaware of the comings and goings of anxious van drivers keeping me informed as vehicles were moved to create a windbreak. Despite such efforts, the flapping grew louder, and I began to hear clanking as the metal poles strained to stay upright and guy ropes tightened as they wrestled to hold them. When gusts started lifting the tent, operation 'calm evacuation' had to be speedily set in motion. I brought the music group back on stage and had everyone file out singing. Fortunately, we'd encouraged parents to stay with their children, and this helped enormously as many had cars parked on site. Everyone else headed for a few of the smaller administration tents that seemed less at risk. By mid-afternoon everyone had made their way home, but as I left the heath the 3,000-seater tent was a soggy, sagging mess, with its canvas ripped open and its bent poles exposed to squalls of thrashing rain.

Of course, that was not the end of the story. After a one-night cancellation and a further night's relocation, the tent was sufficiently dried and repaired for a final packed-out evening, but it left the organising committee with a challenge. They could no longer claim that the south-east London assignment had been completed. They had to think ahead. Some weeks later, with the tent stowed away and the site vacated, I was invited to a meeting of the South East London Mission committee to discuss the possibility of repeating the children's event elsewhere. Somehow during that meeting I found the chair of the committee handing over its future chairing to me. When I arrived home and tried to explain this to my wife, Marion, she responded, 'I thought God called you to be a preacher, not an administrator.' I wholeheartedly agreed but said I didn't think they were looking for an administrator, just for someone with a sense of direction and a willingness to point people the right way. I admitted that I might have suggested something like that during the committee's deliberations, but to be honest I was still reeling from the sudden repositioning.

Returning to the Twelve, I'm sure they could remember times when Jesus had prompted them to think strategically. Let me share one such occasion to show you what I mean. At the end of a very full day of teaching, they're anxiously telling Jesus that everyone in the crowd is hungry. Initially, he seems to be putting the task of feeding the masses back onto them. He listens knowingly as they desperately try to calculate how much it'll cost to buy enough bread. Then two of them find a lad with some lunch, and although they think such a small offering seems pointless among so many, they bring him to Jesus. It's both a shock and a relief when Jesus blesses the boy's lunch and has them serve it as he multiplies it in his hands. It's humbling that, when all are fed, they're urged to gather the leftovers to make sure they also have enough to eat.[4] From start to finish it's a lesson in how God's management strategy always out-classes ours.

Standing together on this Pentecost feast day, it's obvious to the Twelve that once again God has been working ahead of them. They haven't had to fix the date or gather the crowd, and they definitely haven't been left at a loss as to what to say. There are plenty of passages in the Hebrew Scriptures to explain everything from the cross to the resurrection, and from the ascension to their early morning empowerment. All that's required of them at this moment is to put the facts into their historic setting and present God's invitation, but even when they do, they'll know that the personal transformation they'll be promising is way beyond their ability to deliver. Peter steps forward to preach. He gains a hearing by picking up on the crowd's jibes of drunkenness. Clearly he spells out why Jesus died, rose again and ascended, emphasising that the gift of the Holy Spirit he's now pouring out is for all who'll call on the name of the Lord. He urges people to demonstrate their repentance and faith by being baptised so they can receive.[5]

The logistics of what happens next, as people line up for baptism, proves that much of what is taking place is being put together by the Twelve on the spur of the moment. By contrast, Peter's persistence with his appeal as members of the crowd begin to move is something he's obviously totally committed to. As he presses home his message,

---

4. Matthew 14:15-21; Mark 6:35-44; Luke 9:12-17; John 6:5-13.
5. Acts 2:14-39.

1. Positioning: The wind and the tent

the number heading off to be baptised increases to 3,000.[6] If he'd not been so convinced that such a massive response was on God's heart, he may have been content with a brief exhortation and a handful of responders. His determination proves that he's caught something of God's agenda and is partnering with God in delivering it. This is what God's positioning is about for all of us. The moment we think we can out-strategise God, we risk missing out on his agenda and wasting our time creating something that neither knows his power nor reflects his heart. The good news is that God will always seek to steer us away from such tendencies.

Weighing up my unexpected repositioning in the weeks that followed, I realised it answered a question God had been stirring in me for a while: Do you want profile or influence? I knew it was a test and I was tempted to answer 'neither', but I sensed that wasn't an option, and that of the two, 'influence' was the better choice. I was just grateful not to find myself answering 'both'. If God wanted me to be a facilitator with influence, that seemed more than enough for me to cope with for many years to come. But as I share this, I'm no longer thinking only about me. I'm thinking about you too. Thanks to the wind, I was starting on a journey, and if the title of this book has fascinated you, it's possible that God is starting you on a new journey too. So this might be a good moment to pause and think things through. If we're serious about allowing God to position us, how might he work to hold us to his agenda?

Let's return to Peter and draw out a few significant moments in his life. Tracking back a year or so before Pentecost we find him and the rest of the Twelve with Jesus at Caesarea in Philippi. Jesus has just told him he's giving him 'the keys of the kingdom of heaven',

---

6. Acts 2:40-41.

and Peter is left struggling to understand what it might mean.[7] We fast forward to Pentecost and see Peter presenting God's invitation at the close of his message. He's looking for repentance and faith, and as the Jewish residents of Jerusalem, and those from the Jewish diaspora, respond, we see the door of the kingdom of heaven open to receive them. It's an amazing sight. The keys of repentance and faith are clearly working as people come into a new relationship with God.[8] But we need to move forward again, across several years, and hear Peter speaking once more, this time at the first council of the Church held in Jerusalem, 'Brothers, you know that some time ago God made a choice among you that the Gentiles might hear from my lips the message of the gospel and believe.'[9] And Peter was right. God had chosen him to open the door of the kingdom of heaven for both Jews and Gentiles, but this statement about him opening the door for the Gentiles doesn't reveal what a close-run thing it actually had been. We go back again, but this time to just a few years after Pentecost, and find Peter visiting Joppa and praying on his host's rooftop.

Peter is hungry and is given a vision. He sees a sheet full of food forbidden under the Jewish Law. A voice tells him to rise and eat, and he protests, 'Surely not, Lord! I have never eaten anything impure or unclean.' The voice replies, 'Do not call anything impure that God has made clean.' The conversation repeats, and then repeats once more. Peter yet again is left puzzled.[10] But in the meantime there's a delegation at the gate. A group has come from further along the coast where a Roman centurion, a Gentile, has been told by an angel to send for Peter. Fortunately, as they arrive, it dawns on Peter what

---

7. Matthew 16:19.
8. Acts 2:38-41.
9. Acts 15:7.
10. Acts 9:43; 10:9-16.

the sheet is all about and he quickly lines up with God's unfolding plan, agreeing to go with them after they've stayed the night.[11]

Next day, in the centurion's house, he discovers yet more evidence of God still being way ahead of him. He's hardly begun his message when the Holy Spirit comes and intervenes, making it absolutely clear that those listening have just passed through the door into the kingdom. God has obviously seen what is going on in their hearts as Peter starts speaking and the keys of repentance and faith turn in every one of their lives.[12] When Peter reports back to his fellow apostles, they're stunned, but instantly recognise the reality of what has happened by saying, 'So then, even to Gentiles God has granted repentance that leads to life.'[13] Later Peter completes the picture by confirming that God 'purified their hearts by faith.'[14] On the rooftop at Joppa, Peter clearly had a strong sense of responsibility and a determination to engage his brain before he acted, but he had to lay his own conclusions aside and see the need for a humble appreciation of God's sovereignty. If God is ever going to be able to use us to truly help fulfil his strategy (and for Peter, having these two gospel-preaching 'firsts' assigned to him was truly phenomenal) we have to accept that it's God and not we who'll always be the agenda-setter.

I'll return to my own story to underscore the point and to earth it in a more recent setting. It's obvious that I'd yet to see where God was taking me, and apparently God was in less of a hurry than I was to make things really clear. In some ways it was just a case of taking the most obvious next steps while waiting to see where I was heading. But what I thought would be just a few steps while waiting

---

11. Acts 10:1-8, 17-23.
12. Acts 10:23-48.
13. Acts 11:18.
14. Acts 15:9.

turned out to be many, many more. We re-ran the children's day and changed the name of the South East London Mission Committee to South East London Link. We established borough representatives in Greenwich, Lewisham, Bexley and Bromley so we could deepen interchurch relations through joint prayer and shared information. Then, as the mission moved to its central London venue, I found myself being asked to use the knowledge I'd gained locally to help ensure that those responding centrally to the nightly gospel appeals were referred to appropriate participating churches right across the capital.

Nearer to home, we as a church were making some changes. Like many churches at the time, we'd not really considered including small groups in our weekly programme. As many of the ministers I was contacting about the new believers referred to them by the Blackheath mission were also unsure how to run the small groups needed to fulfil the mission's follow-up plan, Marion and I decided to run a series of training courses based on our experience of starting a church in our home.[15] But even as we were sharing our early experiences, I became aware of a south-London-based network of churches, led by someone I greatly respected, that was beginning to advocate a cell-congregation-celebration structure that expected congregations to divide and replicate once they'd reached 120 members. I could see the wisdom of this from a church proliferation perspective, but our church started as a group the size of a cell and had grown into a congregation. Should our next move be to divide the church and create new cells that could grow into further congregations?

---

15. See *Unstoppable Church* (Malcolm Down Publishing, 2024).

1. Positioning: The wind and the tent

Tempting though it was to set time aside to think this through, our church's summer outreach programme needed planning. The students due to be joining us for the week would expect daily Bible teaching sessions, as well as a full timetable of events for children, teens and adults. For some reason I found myself weighing up what biblical model of church I could teach on and opted for Ephesus, simply because it seemed to be the church that cropped up more often in the New Testament than most others. As I prepared my talks, I was fascinated by the fact that the Ephesian church wasn't just a local congregation, it was a church that was able to carry a regional commitment and provide a base for Paul as a global missionary strategist. By contrast, and on a far, far smaller scale, I'd recently had to set up a separate charity for my ministry to students to prevent my local church being overloaded. I began to wonder if there could be an Ephesian way of doing church where the congregation holds a truly wide vision and serves as a resource base for other ministry. If so, how did that fit with the cell-congregation-celebration model that I was now having to consider?

However, at this point I was beginning to get ahead of myself, and possibly even risking running ahead of God's schedule. So, perhaps unsurprisingly, God intervened with an invitation that would re-pace me, and turn my waiting time into something more focused.

Through my work with South East London Link I'd been serving on a small group brought together by the Evangelical Alliance in the wake of the mission to look at establishing a London-wide evangelical fellowship. Someone around the table flippantly said to me, 'Now you've set up South East London Link you've only got to get your head around the other three-quarters of London and you'll have the whole picture.' Maybe that drifted into the ears of the Billy Graham Evangelistic Association's staff team as it considered following up their Mission England tour with a London-based mission. I was invited to handle the anticipated London-wide follow-up!

Believe it or not, my response was to decline the invitation, preferring to stay with something more familiar. But the God who sorted out Peter's dismissiveness in Joppa didn't let me get away with my dismissiveness either. So, reflect on this question and then read on.

Question:

What evidence do you see of God having worked sovereignly in your life to position you?

2. Waiting: *Finding a focus*

Sometimes when significant events are being filmed a cameraman will pan round and capture his fellow photographers in the press pack. It quickly becomes obvious that his colleagues are working with a selection of interchangeable lenses, usually replacing shorter ones with longer ones so they can get close-up shots from a distance. There can be advantages, though, in replacing a close-up lens with a wide-angle one, not just to vary the shot but to provide more context. When God is preparing us for an assignment, he often takes us through multiple lens changes while we wait. He wants to make sure we understand the wider picture of what he's leading us into as well as seeing it close to. To show how this works, we'll start to look at Paul's assignment and his early days of preparation. I'll also share something of how God used my waiting time to give me a more realistic grasp of what he knew lay ahead for me. I hope these two accounts will be an encouragement to you if and when you find yourself moving from positioning to waiting.

As I ended the last chapter admitting that I'd retreated to my safety zone when given the opportunity to gain more experience, I'd better explain why that safety zone had such a strong appeal for me. It wasn't that it would give me more time to plan for an Ephesus-style church; I hadn't reached that far in my thinking. It was just that from my early twenties I'd been building a student ministry among Christian Unions in universities, colleges and medical schools based on strong personal relationships. I had no illusions. I reckoned the reason I was invited back more often than most speakers had more to do with my willingness to stay late and drink coffee than any depth of wisdom I may have shared in my talks. But this relational way of doing things meant I was maintaining my usefulness year on year by getting to know new students as they arrived. I could see that a few years of whole-hearted commitment to a capital-wide mission would probably end my student connections once and for all. I was more than a little reluctant to move on. It took a vision for Peter to let go of his narrow focus. It was a handshake that did it for me.

Marion and I were asked to an event where Billy Graham was going to express his thanks to the churches inviting him to London. For him the greeting and thanking were standard practice, but as he shook my hand and thanked me for accepting the student mobilisation role that someone had just whispered I was planning to play, a question cropped up in my mind that knocked me sideways: How could I be thinking, 'How little can I give?' As he held my gaze and gripped my hand, I decided to volunteer for everything that was asked of me. I ended up not only agreeing to oversee the follow-up but agreeing to head-up the counselling too, working virtually full-time for a year-and-a-half as the mission spread out nationally and internationally. It had only taken seconds for the lens of my life to change and my vision to widen dramatically. With eighteen months of busyness now ahead of me I think we can pause and dig more deeply into the link between Peter's breakthrough in the centurion's house and the early years of Paul's ministry while he's still called Saul. We'll see that there's a lot more to lining up with God's agenda than simply jumping on the back of the latest craze. In fact God often expects some of us to get on board with a project long before it has gathered any momentum, let alone become the one thing everyone wants to be seen joining.

2. Waiting: Finding a focus

Neither on the Jerusalem road nor in Straight Street has God left Saul in any doubt that his mission will be to the Gentiles.[16] This has its challenges. Before meeting Jesus, Saul was as Gentile-cautious as Peter. Now he's straining to get started on this new cross-cultural calling. He tells himself that deep down he's always known that when God chose Abraham to be a blessing to the nations it showed that the Gentiles had always been on God's heart.[17] Now he's a man with a mission looking for a strategy. He knows it's early days and that he's still a work in progress, but he can clearly see the theological obstacles he needs to overcome. What's more, as far as he's aware, given that Peter's rooftop vision is still in the future, there's no Jewish believer who has yet reached out to the Gentiles, other than to those Gentiles who'd already made Judaism their own.[18] He's going to have to tackle this assignment without anyone other than God to guide him. He has to accept, as we all do, that God is just as passionate about those to whom he gives an assignment as he is about the assignment itself. Our fears around being ill-equipped and recruited too early have to be laid aside.

Damascus gives Saul some breathing space. He ministers to the Jewish diaspora alongside Ananias, probably wondering, as a trained Pharisee, how strict he should be in applying the Law.[19] He knows that, given his calling and his new-found sense of personal liberty, it's a question he'll have to answer. The Roman province of Arabia is close by, lying to the east and south of Damascus,[20] and it looks as if it could offer him the personal space he needs to think and pray. He heads off, determined to stay there until God makes things clear. His

---

16. Acts 26:12-18; 9:11-17; 22:6-16.
17. Genesis 12:1-3.
18. Acts 2:11.
19. Acts 9:19-22.
20. The Roman province of Arabia took in much of what is now modern Syria and the Sinai Peninsula.

active brain is seeking theological answers, but when they come they bring a greater awareness of the awesomeness of God.[21] He returns to Damascus to let his new understanding sink in. But things change quickly. Aretas, the regional ruler whose territory includes Damascus, wants Saul arrested. The believers in Damascus draw on their ingenuity (and a basket) to help him escape.[22]

Three years have passed since Saul was last in Jerusalem and memories of the persecution he let loose have stayed in people's minds. News of his arrival makes some people uneasy, but he shows his boldness by preaching in a Jewish community that at one time would have welcomed him. It now greets him with murderous threats, and Barnabas and Peter, the two local leaders he's been spending most time with, believe the wisest thing for him to do is to move back to his home area. There are bound to be plenty of opportunities to preach to Gentiles in Cilicia.[23] But as he goes, we must ask ourselves a question: how much success will he have before Peter makes his God-ordained visit to a Gentile household? The answer could be 'very little'.

Given Saul's temperament, it's easy to imagine him quickly setting to work around Tarsus. Clearly Peter has never spoken to him about his double door-opening assignment. In all probability Peter hasn't yet grasped the fullness of it himself. So no one can blame Saul for assuming the door's wide open and throwing himself wholeheartedly into preaching and teaching. The personal suffering that comes his way is overwhelming. Later, when writing to the Corinthians, he lists some of the things that happen during this period.[24] It's ridiculously tough, but suddenly, as he presses on

---

21. Galatians 1:16-17.
22. 2 Corinthians 11:32-33; Acts 9:23-25.
23. Acts 9:26-30; Galatians 1:18-24.
24. 2 Corinthians 11:23-27.

2. Waiting: Finding a focus

undaunted, something shifts. Cornelius's house is too far away for him to know where it started, but I guess he just sees the Gentiles in Cilicia becoming more responsive to his preaching. At the same time, unbeknown to him, some Cypriot believers in neighbouring Syria are successfully planting a church in Antioch that includes Gentiles. When the church in Jerusalem sends Barnabas to Antioch to encourage them, Barnabas, being Saul's personal encourager-of-old, seeks him out to have him join the team.[25] Clearly it's a new era and yet somehow, in the purposes of God, I believe Saul's determination throughout his early days in Cilicia contributed to the breakthrough. God never wastes people's passionate praying and well-directed, fervent activity.

I find reflecting on Saul's time in Cilicia particularly helpful when I'm having to encourage early adopters who are mystified by matters of timing, and in the past I've had to encourage myself with Saul's realities too. Unexpected delays can definitely be the result of unknown issues beyond our control. But there are some matters we can control that will help our development. I'll mention three, and stay with my illustration of looking through different lenses. The points I'll highlight are: increasing capacity, appreciating support and expanding knowledge.

Working on a large-scale, stadium-based mission is exciting, but being brought onto the team early can quickly open up a world where tasks expand beyond expectations, hard work behind the scenes offers no immediate rewards and the things you think you know well have to be revisited.

I expected a gentle lead in to my new role, especially as the training programme to equip church members for the mission was

---

25. Acts 11:19-26.

on someone else's schedule. My training responsibilities for follow-up were to come later. I'd worked long hours before and knew God could keep providing the energy, but some aspects of multitasking (or, perhaps more accurately, the art of keeping multiple plates spinning) had yet to come my way. When the church leader assigned to work alongside me as chair of counselling found his personal timetable overloaded, his role was added to mine. At the same time live video links were announced to take place across the nation, and the training programmes expanded from London-wide to nationwide. My wide-angle lens had suddenly got wider, but I didn't want to miss out on close-ups. It occurred to me that two London churches deserved special attention; one had as its rector the chair of the mission and the other had as its senior minister the person I was replacing as chair of counselling. Keen to set an example, I taught the training classes at All Souls, Langham Place, and Kensington Temple. For two nights each week, as the courses ran nationally, I enjoyed exchanging a wide-angle lens for a close-up one.

I saw echoes of Saul's determination in this period leading up to the mission. I'd never entertained the idea of being an armchair strategist but Saul performed unstintingly, not only when being written about by Luke but when hidden from the biblical record. Nothing he did in his years in Cilicia appears in the book of Acts,[26] but Barnabas seems to have had no trouble finding him. Throughout that Cilicia period he was probably labouring alone. It was his subsequent experience of serving as a team member at Antioch that led him to adopt a shared leadership model for the rest of his life.[27] He wanted people alongside him rather than under him, and preferred

---

26. As mentioned earlier, perhaps the best glimpse of his time in Cilicia comes from the list of personal disasters in 2 Corinthians 11:23-27. Maybe also from some of the names listed in Romans before he'd ever visited Rome.
27. Acts 13:1.

2. Waiting: Finding a focus

people to share the load with him rather than lift it completely off him. As I was switching my focus backwards and forwards between setting up the counselling and preparing the follow-up, I eventually got around to using Saul's principles and gathered groups around me to help me handle everything counselling-related and everything follow-up related. I couldn't have managed without these task-related teams, or the wider teams I myself was part of.

In the midst of all this I was seeing my grasp of follow-up and church mobilisation as my strongest points. It's said that London taxi drivers know the capital by its streets, pubs and tourist attractions. Thanks to the previous mission, I knew London by its mission-minded churches. I was good at marking them with pins on a map, but I needed to expand my knowledge and find out what was actually happening around the pins. The mission was eventually held in four locations: West Ham, Crystal Palace, Earls Court and Wembley, and understanding local social conditions and geography proved vital. I wasn't sure what I was going to do with my increasing knowledge in the long-term but it was serving me well in the moment.

The mission reached its highpoint in a final one-off event at Wembley, and although it wasn't my personal finishing point, it provides an opportunity to tell just one of many stories destined to stay with me.

I'm standing at Billy Graham's famous adjustable pulpit. (It seems to guess your height as you approach it.) I've been asked to take the offering at Crystal Palace and the privilege of announcing 'We're going to Wembley' has fallen to me. If that's not enough, on the big day a week or so later, I find myself sitting on the platform. This proves to be a challenge as it's pouring with rain and the cover over the platform doesn't extend far enough to protect the backs of those of us in the very back row. But there's a bigger challenge. While Billy

Graham is preaching I'm thinking ahead to the counselling. Having thousands of individuals we've trained talking with everyone who publicly responds is relatively easy in the dry, but this is our biggest crowd, our heaviest downpour and the lack of umbrellas is clear for all to see. Not only am I unable to access my deputy but I have no way of engaging with Billy Graham who, at the end of his sermon, will be asking people to leave their seats and stand on the pitch.

As the preaching hits home, my back is getting wetter and wetter and my brain is working harder and harder. Billy Graham seems unfazed. He makes his appeal and my heart is in my mouth. But the moment the first person steps onto the pitch the rain stops. The whole experience is truly moving. When I come off the stage to supervise, the pitch is like a paddy field waiting for the shoots of rice to emerge, but no one is put off. There are just a few among the 3,000 plus responders who've come to Wembley simply to stand on the pitch. They find themselves being counselled along with everyone else. The privilege of witnessing all of this is well worth the cost of a replacement suit. Seeing people come into Christ's kingdom is priceless.

For me the mission wound down slowly. Across the weeks from West Ham to Wembley we'd had a team of up to 1,200 working through the night to allocate people to churches and a further team working through the day. The day team continued with me for several months after the mission, making sure that the responders from all four venues were referred appropriately to one of our 1,500 participating churches. But just as things were beginning to quieten down and my head and heart were ready to process all I'd learnt, unexpected ministry opportunities forced me to stop and make a decision.

2. Waiting: Finding a focus

A church in west London and two in central London wanted me on staff, and a church in my home town was making an approach to me about taking on its leadership. Make-up-my-mind time had arrived at a moment when I least expected it. Should I just dismiss what God had started stirring in me before the mission about an Ephesus-style church, or should I have it central in my thinking as I try to discern the way ahead? I could see that ignoring those past stirrings wasn't really an option, and although I believed God had been deliberately giving me little free time in which to overthink things, I'd seen throughout the two missions that there were signs that London could be opening up to change, and for me to be part of a church that was keen to have a wider remit would make sense.

I know that in sharing this story of my personal waiting period, I've almost certainly taken you down a path that is totally different from the one God may use to give you your focus. My eyes were being opened to London. God may want to open your eyes to very different opportunities and challenges. Even so, I was still keeping my family in sight, and faced with four options Marion and I settled matters together. Having supported each other as I'd maintained my hectic pace for eighteen months, we knew that now was not the time for us to be relocating. We needed to stay put for the sake of the children's schooling. We decided that I should talk to the elders of the local church that had approached me, and raise the possibility of a merger rather than a transfer of leadership. Somewhere in my thinking I hoped that we could produce a new Ephesus-style church in the suburbs, capable, like All Souls and Kensington Temple, of having a wider vision and wider impact.

Before finalising my decision I went to talk to the south-London leader who'd triggered my thinking with his cell-congregation-celebration model. How would he feel about my bucking his trend by seeking to raise a sizeable congregation in south London similar to some churches in the centre? He didn't give me a direct answer but took our conversation off at a tangent by saying, 'We need younger leaders on our central committees, and I think, given your student work and your mission experience, you can help us achieve it.' The concept of every leader having a 'Timothy' was not new to me, but the idea of giving a Timothy equal status was different, perhaps a bit more like having a Silas.[28] My interest was piqued. I'd enjoyed working in partnerships before and loved the idea of once again making room for a younger person in ministry.

As I finish this chapter on waiting, we must leave Paul and Silas for the moment and start talking about Aquila and Priscilla, the married couple who made tents and became the founding partnership for the Ephesian church.[29] For many of us, as we go forward, this couple will be more valuable as role models than Paul and Silas. When Marion and I were working closely on our first church plant, we loved the equality of Aquila and Priscilla's relationship. The Bible even at times dispenses with the conventions of the day, referring to them as Priscilla and Aquila.[30] But for now it's just Aquila's name I want to borrow. His name means eagle and in a couple of sentences I want to use it to sum up my thoughts on multiple lenses. The eagle's eye perfectly illustrates the point. An eagle can fly high and take in an incredible overview while maintaining the pinpoint accuracy that enables it to swoop down in response to the slightest ground-level movement. I'm sure that for every one of us there is a place for both the wide-angle view and the close-up as God prepares us for our assignment.

---

28. Acts 15:22, 40; 16:19-25.
29. Acts 18:1-3.
30. Acts 18:26.

So having looked at waiting, we now need to think about assessing. We'll do this in the next chapter with the help of Priscilla and Aquila, along with the assistance of a man from Macedonia, and a woman from Thyatira who made her living selling purple cloth.[31]

Question:

Is God exposing you to challenges that are giving you a wider vision while waiting to get into the full flow of your assignment? If so, how are you making the most of them?

---

31. Acts 16:9,14.

3. Assessing: Pictures of hope

Not surprisingly, the main picture printed on my mind as I moved on from my second capital-wide mission in six years was a map of London. I'd come to think of the capital as roughly diamond-shaped with the symmetry skewed by the Outer London boroughs of Havering, Hillingdon and Bromley. There is no way, though, that I could straighten out the path of the Thames. It enters from the south-west and winds its way up to loop across the centre before exiting from the east. The Thames and all thirty-two boroughs, plus the City, were clearly marked in my thinking, but whereas the map in the mission office was covered with pins identifying the participating churches, I now saw the map pin-free, ready for some fresh strategic thinking. And that strategic thinking needed to start right away. The Evangelical Alliance project for London had gained fresh momentum, and my involvement prompted me to analyse the insights I'd been gathering concerning the capital. Interestingly, it was the river that provoked the questions.

To help me, I'm going to place Paul (no longer called Saul) by a river too, as he prepares his chosen assessors for Ephesus. I'm sure it would have been more than tent-making that attracted Paul to Priscilla and Aquila when he first arrived in Corinth. He may have met them as fellow Jews in the synagogue there and, having learned that they shared his trade, rejoiced to see them come to share his faith. By the way, we're never told how Paul acquired his tent-making skills. Did theological students in first-century Jerusalem pay their way through their studies by stitching tents for the Roman

Army? If so, he may have been a bit out of practice when trying to repay Priscilla and Aquila for their generosity as he settled in as their house guest.[32] And if all of this is speculation, so is my thought that from early on in their relationship Paul may have seen them as people he would bring onto his team to prepare the way for him in Ephesus. But that is certainly what he eventually had them do. Maybe he used his time with them in Corinth to equip them for what was to come. If he did, he would have shared with them about his time by the river in Philippi.[33] Let's stretch our imaginations as we work out what Aquila and Priscilla may have learned.

Paul's second mission trip from Antioch has already been a long one. His first trip had been relatively short: a time with Barnabas on Cyprus and then on to Galatia.[34] This time, he and Silas reached Galatia by preaching their way through Cilicia, and it was in Galatia that Paul recruited Timothy. The three then carried on travelling west towards Ephesus on the Aegean coast. But God didn't want them in Asia yet, or for that matter in Bithynia where they tried to enter next. Unsure of where to go, they end-up waiting on the coast at Troas, north of Ephesus, along with a young doctor called Luke who's just joined them. Paul sees a man in a vision calling him to come to Macedonia to help. Although the man doesn't mention a specific city, Paul, thinking strategically, opts for Philippi, a major Macedonian centre.[35] When they arrive he decides, unusually for him, that although there may have been a synagogue in Philippi (there was certainly one in nearby Thessalonica) that he'll start his Macedonian campaign with corporate prayer rather than preaching.

---

32. Acts 18:1-3.
33. Acts 16:12-15.
34. Acts 13:4 – 14:26.
35. Acts 15:40 – 16:12.

3. Assessing: Pictures of hope

Luke (whom Paul has now left in Philippi) writes a note in his diary, which makes Paul smile as he recalls it:

On the Sabbath we went outside the city gate to the river, where we expected to find a place of prayer. We sat down and began to speak to the women who had gathered there.[36]

I think that at this point in the story Priscilla and Aquila would have been smiling too, finding the thought of fellow pray-ers, especially female ones, particularly encouraging. For Paul, he's probably just delighted to remember the joy of getting alongside people who, like the man in the vision, were showing a concern for their region, even though they hadn't yet had an opportunity to respond to the gospel.

Now I'm going to pause at this point because, for me, my encouragement lay in the fact that Paul knew exactly where to look for these pray-ers, and that it was by a river. Praying by a river is a picture that still fills me with hope and I'm convinced that hope is essential for every one of us when taking on a new assignment. I'm sure we can all think of Old Testament prophets who were called to pronounce God's judgement. I don't envy them the challenge of maintaining their ministry in the face of such a predetermined outcome.[37] Sometimes we may have to make positive declarations while we're weeping inside, and there's nothing wrong with that if our positive words and inner brokenness are both from God. We should be cautious, though, if we find ourselves reinforcing negative declarations with our own inbuilt negativity. In Romans 15:5 God is described as the giver of 'endurance and encouragement'. Coming to terms with an assignment will always involve seeing things that

---

36. Acts 16:13.
37. Isaiah 6:8-13.

need to change. Having a picture of hope embedded in our minds will enable us to more authentically offer hope to those around us.

And so to the river, and let me admit that I really have no idea why Lydia and her friends decided to pray beside a river. If asked, they may have replied 'privacy', 'peacefulness' or simply 'convenience', but I'd like to think there was also an element of inspiration. For me, a river flowing through a city can prompt three questions: What things have been brought in that should be kept? What things have been brought in that should be shared more widely? What things have been brought in that need to be flushed out? Any prayer meeting anywhere can ask these questions, regardless of whether or not there is a physical river in the town. In reality, seeing the river as a picture of hope has less to do with any inspiration that may come from Philippi's river, or in my case, the Thames, and far more to do with Revelation 22:1-2:

> Then the angel showed me the river of the water of life, as clear as crystal, flowing from the throne of God and of the Lamb down the middle of the great street of the city. On each side of the river stood the tree of life, bearing twelve crops of fruit, yielding its fruit every month. And the leaves of the tree are for the healing of the nations.

If this river were to flow in full spate through our cities and assignments, transformation would be guaranteed. We need all that flows from the throne of God and we need the tree of life available in every street of what would become our well-watered communities. We also need the river to carry leaves of healing to the nations in our strife-torn world.

3. Assessing: Pictures of hope

We move on and catch up with a well-briefed Aquila and Priscilla accompanying Paul as he leaves Corinth. After almost two years of preaching and teaching there, he's heading for Antioch via Jerusalem, but they'll be stopping at Ephesus on route. The three of them board a ship at the port of Cenchrea, a few miles east of Corinth, and cross the Aegean Sea to enter the wide delta of the river Kaysos with the city of Ephesus spreading out before them. The river meanders off to the north before heading east, but Paul leaves Aquila and Priscilla on the quayside to sort out accommodation while he heads off to find the synagogue where he intends to engage with the congregation. He knows this for him will be a short trip but he has to settle Aquila and Priscilla. After a few days he's ready to move on but those gathering at the synagogue are pressing him to stay longer. Despite almost certainly having long-held hopes for Ephesus, he replies cautiously about a possible return. He wants to make sure he stays in line with God's plan. As his ship sails for Caesarea, Aquila and Priscilla find themselves on their own, ready to take stock of the area while praying for Paul's return.[38]

As I try to answer my three river questions in London, I'll set out what I think might have been Aquila and Priscilla's likely responses for Ephesus. They're in a city the Greeks had built about a thousand years earlier on a previously inhabited site. Being a port, it's acquired a multicultural population. Paul has already met the Jewish community. There's unmissable evidence of the current Roman rule, which the residents seem to be accepting. It's still a wealthy city and the capital of the province. It feels very Greek, and Greek is the common language.[39] All of these seem to be things that are around

---

38. Acts 18:18-21.
39. This was true for most of the Roman Empire, following on as it did from the empire of Alexander the Great.

to stay, but what Aquila and Priscilla will truly be wanting to see stay and expand is the response to the gospel, evident after Paul's few days of preaching in the synagogue. The interest that's been created is something they'll build on through personal relationships at the synagogue, even though they won't be taking on Paul's public preaching role.

By comparison, London's early days as part of the Roman Empire have been followed by influxes of different people groups across two millennia. It has become a truly diverse and multicultural city. It's had its tensions but the potential for harmony and generosity of spirit are great. Communication technologies are developing and transport links within and without are generally good, making London as accessible in our day as Ephesus must have seemed to Aquila and Priscilla. Furthermore, as I was making my assessment I'd just witnessed a decade with some significant response to the gospel and I'm definitely believing for more.

Communication-wise, Ephesus is a city that for at least a century has been regarded by wealthy Greeks as a travel destination. Its Temple of Artemis, initially completed in 550 BC, is regarded as one of the seven wonders of the world. Travel and trading links are good, and, being a provincial capital, engagement across the province works well too. The river that creates the harbour contributes to transporting goods and enabling exports, all of which helps raise the city's profile. It really is a hub city, so what happens in Ephesus can soon spread far and wide.

As I continued to look at London, I was ticking many of the same boxes, especially when it came to ease of spreading information. For Ephesus there were certainly commercial and architectural skills that could be shared, and as the city seemed to be well administered and prospering, maybe there was diplomatic expertise that could

3. Assessing: Pictures of hope

be passed on to other places seeking to thrive under Rome. But the main thing for Aquila and Priscilla would be the potential for spreading the good news of Christ's reconciling death and life-giving resurrection. Given that the connectivity throughout the Roman Empire, and the widespread use of Greek, are helping everyone everywhere to circulate ideas, surely conditions are ideal for the spread of the gospel, with Ephesus being a great base from which to share.

Part of the proof of this concept of easy spread lies in its then-current ability to mobilise the whole region in Diana worship.[40] The entwining of the identities of the Greek goddess Artemis and the Roman goddess Diana have added to the significance of the Ephesus Temple. The trade in charms and occult religious material is a major feature of local life and costs dutiful residents a fortune. Unravelling this will mean that there is much work for the gospel to do. And if that is not enough, the Jewish community has its own exorcists trying to deal with spiritual forces that are clearly disturbing the people in the area. They're not solving the problems, but add spiritual confusion to the already existing issues of inequality, abuse and potential for social unrest.

I had my mixture of hopes and concerns for London too, and was keen to see a tidal wave of God's word bringing life and cleansing to its problems. But it was a time when many church leaders were being incredibly pessimistic about the capital, speaking of an oppressive cloud hanging over the city. I mentioned this to a visiting minister from Asia and his response was wonderfully refreshing. 'The only cloud I see over London,' he said, 'is a cloud of blessing, laid up over the city through hundreds of years of faithful gospel preaching, just

---

40. Acts 19:27.

reach up and release its downpour.' With a river and downpour in mind I came back to my London map.

There were times in past centuries when the Thames would have been hard pressed to generate a picture of hope as it flowed through England's capital. Instead of removing pollution from the city, it became the city's chief polluter. When engineers created covered sewers along its banks, the environment improved dramatically. Much was then done to clean the river even further. More remains to be done, but as I look at the Houses of Parliament, the hospitals, schools, parks, museums, art galleries, tourist attractions, institutions and expensive apartment blocks along its banks, I long for the real river of life to touch every one of them.

Sadly, the river Kaysos at Ephesus also caused more problems than it solved, as the silt it carried from inland increasingly clogged the port. Dredging the delta helped,[41] but the silting continued and eventually the floodplains that created the delta became a swamp. Now, in the twenty-first century, the river enters the sea further along the coast and the ruins of Ephesus stand five miles inland. I think both the Thames and the Kaysos may have something to say to us as we hold onto the hope of Revelation 22.

As assessing often goes hand-in-hand with waiting, there is one more lesson we can learn from the riverside prayer meetings in Philippi. It's from the unusual story of Paul waiting to bring deliverance to a girl who has followed him and his team for days, shouting, 'These men are servants of the Most High God, who are telling you the way to be saved.'[42] It sounded great but the spirit from which it was coming was wrong. Paul would have known

---

41. Some seventy years before Aquila and Priscilla arrived in Ephesus, Mark Anthony had assembled a massive fleet in the harbour.
42. Acts 16:16-24.

3. Assessing: Pictures of hope

this immediately but must have realised that she was a victim who needed handling with care. He obviously wasn't worried about his personal safety (he and Silas ended up in prison anyway), but there were concerns about what her owners might do to her once she'd lost her clairvoyant 'gift' and was no longer useful to them. Before he sets her free, he makes sure there is a caring community to surround her. Not everyone is as wise as Paul in taking account of wider circumstances. No doubt Aquila and Priscilla would have picked this up in their earlier training in Corinth, adding to their growing understanding of Paul.

We have no way of knowing if Aquila and Priscilla have finished assessing the challenges in and around Ephesus when Apollos comes to the synagogue and speaks about the ministry of John the Baptist. His arrival for them is a real sign of hope as they continue to pray for Paul's return. They come into their own when counselling him and establishing him in the truth about Jesus. They may not know about the small group of followers in the city who'd been baptised purely on a public confession of sin rather than on identification with Christ's death and resurrection. The privilege of helping them will go to Paul on his arrival. He'll baptise them and see them empowered by the Holy Spirit. Meanwhile Aquila and Priscilla are happy to agree to the request from Apollos to be sent to Corinth knowing that he will be going there truly empowered by God. I'm sure it's a mixed blessing for them as they would no doubt love to have Apollos alongside them for the remaining weeks before Paul's return. But the generosity with which they give, not only adds some urgency to their prayers for Paul's return but is met by God's even greater generosity in not only giving them Paul but by providing a starting point for the work with the twelve that Apollos left behind.[43]

---

43. Acts 18:24 – 19:7.

As I put everything together in the weeks following the mission, I, like Apollos, was keen to move on, not from Ephesus but towards it. My Ephesian church model was now convincing me that a local commitment could link with a wider regional vision and I was at last ready to share my hope for capital transformation, not only on a London-wide platform but with what I expected would soon be my expanded home congregation.

Things were to prove more difficult than I anticipated but sometimes that's the consequence of having convinced yourself that with the assessment completed, the waiting must already be over.

Question:

What picture of hope do you have in mind for the locality, or area of work, in which you believe God will have you serve him?

4. Sharing: *Gaining a hearing*

If you type 'overwinding a clockwork clock' into a search engine you'll get a selection of answers. Some will say it's impossible to do; others will say you might break the spring. I think that at least one of the two stories I'm about to tell proves it's possible to break the spring. But I want to set the tone for this chapter on vision-sharing by giving some context around how tightly wound I may have become myself, even though I was not aware of it at the time. I'm sharing as openly as I can so that you can bring whatever balance you may feel is necessary to the two stories I'm about to share. Here is some context.

While the Graham mission was taking place, a prominent Christian statistician conducted an English Church Census. The facts and figures were published to inspire church leaders to take the Church forward by becoming strategic thinkers. I studied his analysis while I was looking for a picture of hope for London and was fascinated to discover he saw hope in the leadership style of some of my friends and contacts. He labelled them as 'Pioneers of the House Church Movement', reflecting the term by which we, as leaders of new independent churches, were known at the time. His exact quote was

As someone once said, 'Things only get done by mono-maniacs on a mission'. The Pioneers of the House Church Movement, like . . . [and he listed six leaders I knew well], could be so described. One imagines that their motto might easily have been that of Hannibal when facing the Pyrenees on his elephants, 'I will find a way across or make one'.[44]

I loved the alliteration of mono-maniacs on a mission and wondered if the term applied to me as much as to them. After the second capital-wide mission, Marion and I took a week off to walk in one of the most beautiful valleys in the Lake District. The scenery was therapeutic but my mind was still busy, looking for ways I could push myself forward further and faster. I wasn't too bothered about Hannibal and his elephants but if being a mono-maniac with a mission was what it would take to get things done, so be it.

To be honest, I'd been so much in my element during the missions that I probably wouldn't have welcomed any well-meaning person telling me to take things more slowly. Now that I was gaining a vision for a transformed London and an Ephesus-style church, I was excited to see that fulfilled too. But although I'd proved that God can supply the energy to keep me going, it never crossed my mind to ask anyone if in telling the Colossians, 'I strenuously contend with all the energy Christ so powerfully works in me', Paul was encouraging everyone to become as zealously focused as I was.[45] Maybe I should have paused and asked myself that question.

Looking back I can see that God had his safeguards in place. Being acknowledged as part of a generation of pioneering hope-bringers on the front edge of the charismatic renewal was encouraging, but it created some elements of unreality. We were certainly overstating the case when we began to regard ourselves as spiritually fatherless, simply because some who'd gone before us expressed doubts about

---

44. Peter Brierley, *'Christian' England: what the 1989 English Church Census reveals* (London: MARC Europe, 1991), p. 46. The original 'mono-maniac' quote is not cited but can be found in the literature of the business world at the time. The Hannibal quote is normally given in Latin: *'aut viam inveniam aut faciam'*.
45. Colossians 1:29; Galatians 4:18.

aspects of our charismatic theology. The upside to this was that we formed strong relationships with each other, but I believe that there were father figures graciously giving us space, praying for us, protecting us and cheering us on our way, if only from the side-lines. I wish now that I'd recognised this.

Now that I've set the scene, the vision-sharing story I'll cover first is the London-wide one, although in reality the London-wide and local stories unfolded side-by-side. I'll begin with the Evangelical Alliance.

Having set out to establish a London-wide evangelical fellowship after the first mission, the EA was even more determined to build on the increased momentum following the Graham campaign. An EA staff member and I were asked to take on the task. After many planning meetings we recommended that the borough committees set up for the Graham mission should continue, and be encouraged to engage with their local government bodies, the London borough councils. We thought this was a good way to effect social change. At first the idea was met with enthusiasm and we were asked to draft a template for rolling out Local Evangelical Fellowships nationally. In the end, though, it was an idea that went nowhere as some key people saw it as possibly conflicting with CARE Trust's recently launched national initiative to set up constituency groups to impact central government in Westminster.[46] When we were given the opportunity to address a one-off London-wide leaders' meeting convened jointly by the Evangelical Alliance and CARE, the response to my presentation on the need for a London-wide

---

46. CARE – Christian, Action, Research and Education – is a member body of the Evangelical Alliance that was set up to engage with the Westminster government on political issues following the Nationwide Festival of Light in 1971. Most London boroughs at the time had two or three parliamentary constituencies within their borders.

vision was mixed. Some believed that, despite the mission's success with its borough-by-borough approach, churches coalesce more naturally along local lines and vision should be kept at that level. Sadly, overall, it seemed that grasping a London-wide vision was something few were interested in.

Graciously, the leaders of the Evangelical Alliance and CARE settled for a regular London Leaders' Prayer Meeting and I found myself on its organising committee. I chose not to see this as a setback, interpreting it instead as an important step towards keeping the London-wide vision alive while giving others the opportunity to buy into it. I was having to learn that it's God who sets the pace, and that patient persistence may have to continue for longer than anticipated. And now for the even more challenging story, the local one.

Having weighed the request from the nearby church and pointed out to the leaders who had approached me that I was not prepared to leave one church to take on another, I met with a Christian solicitor to see what a merger might involve. He studied both churches' governing documents and proposed that each church should begin the process by voting on three statements: 1. that I should be the minister of both churches, 2. that the two churches should share the same building, and 3. that the two churches should work towards becoming one. This was accepted by the leaders of both churches and we agreed to vote on the same day. The membership of the two churches was numerically similar, although the church making the approach had a larger attendance. The church I was already leading returned a ninety-seven per cent 'yes' on all three points, and the word came through that the result at the other church was pretty much the same. Furthermore, we were told that its members were looking forward to my induction service within a few weeks

4. Sharing: Gaining a hearing

and were keen to share their building while we looked for larger premises, something they'd been considering for some time.

In no time at all I was inducted and the two churches were meeting together in the larger church's building. One of the things that thrilled those I was newly working with was that they'd been told by a visiting speaker they would double in size within a year. Amazingly, they had seen it happen in the space of a single Sunday morning service. The church building was quickly reordered to fit everybody in, and I wasted no time in preparing a booklet setting out who was who in each church and providing a schedule of the combined churches' weekly events. The booklet also gave some indication as to how the different teams in the merging churches would be working together. But much of this seemed to be taking the premises-owning church by surprise. I put it down to a change of leadership style and the fact that it was the first time some were finding out who did what from among their own congregation. We pressed on together and saw further growth as news of our amalgamation spread.

Understandably, there were teething problems. Some long-term members of the resident church struggled with feeling cramped in their newly reconfigured premises, but, despite this, I was sufficiently encouraged to start talking about combining our governing documents. I set aside a Saturday when anyone from either church could come and share their thoughts with me. It turned out to be a strange day that left me with a sense of unease. Some people knew nothing about the churches merging and asked basic questions about what was going on. Even some of the trustees of the resident church had no idea what was intended and sent the draft constitution that we'd begun discussing off to their denominational headquarters. As the day drew to a close it seemed that, apart from the two elders who originally approached me, the only ones who really knew what was going on were those from my original church, and some of the visionary-minded young people from the resident church who had worked out that we must have come together for some purpose other than just uniting for unity's sake. Although everyone knew of my wider involvements, future plans for us all to begin to think more widely were hardly mentioned.

Tensions were creeping in. While the pace of change was exciting for some, it was clearly disturbing for others. Even the basic changes that were needed to cope with the increase in numbers and the combining of activities were proving difficult to put in place. Close questioning at a combined elders' meeting exposed the problem: the resident church was never given the opportunity to vote on the three points. They'd simply been told, 'Hugh is willing to come and will bring 200 people with him' (even the number was slightly exaggerated in the midst of what no doubt was a well-meant miscommunication). A few weeks later, when an opportunity for personal testimonies was provided in the Sunday service, the previous minister stood to bring a short word of encouragement. While sharing, he disclosed the date he decided to retire. I noted it was after the date that the initial approaches were made to me. It was a shock, but a few days later I had a pleasant surprise. As a result of the trustees' referral of the new draft governing documents, I was visited by a team from the denominational headquarters who had travelled to London specially to talk to me and express their gratitude. Evidently the newest minister on their ministerial accreditation pathway (namely me) had spotted an inconsistency in the denomination's governing documents at exactly the same moment as the Charity Commission had brought it to their attention. All of this was a lot for me to take in, but as the previous minister and his wife were still in the church,

I decided to take the two of them into my confidence and draw on their advice as I worked things through. I could see that, through my lack of awareness, I had been trying to re-envision those who were already committed to a very different goal. I needed to find a way of gently unwinding my efforts and then to take things forward without breaking the spring. Realistically, options seemed limited.

If I needed evidence that my vision-sharing with the resident church was not going well, I didn't have to wait long. Its members held a members' meeting without informing me. When I found out I sympathised with their expressions of pain. In their minds they had shown a lot of graciousness in welcoming others into their building and seemed to feel they were at risk of losing their identity in the process. If only I'd known how little they knew, I would have approached things very differently, taking time to get to know them and doing far more to help them adjust after years of enjoying their previous minister's ministry. The challenge by then, though, was that with six or seven months behind us the combined church was no longer divided along original congregational lines. Some who had come with me were, like me, sharing other people's pain.

One Sunday I asked the previous pastor back to the pulpit. He knew the whole situation and to my surprise preached on sounding the alarm. As I listened I knew that my days were numbered. With our first year drawing to a close, I knew that I was not alone in thinking that the positives had more than outweighed the pains, but I also knew that not everyone saw it that way. I asked the elders if they'd like me to resign and if so when. The answer came back, 'Yes, next Sunday.' A joint members' meeting was convened for the following Monday night, and with the prior agreement of the leadership teams of both churches I explained the way forward. The plan was not to unravel the merger as many strong personal relationships had been built, but for me to lead a new church plant using the constitution of my original church. Following further advice from the solicitor, I asked the members of my original church at one point during the Monday night meeting to join me in a room on the other side of the car park so I could formally request the continuing use of the constitution.

At the Sunday morning service after the meeting, I repeated all I'd said, but pain was distorting what people were hearing and it was hard to get the message across. Furthermore, those who'd previously formed strong conclusions tended to be reluctant to revise them. There were those from both churches who longed for things to go back to how they were, and those from both churches who wanted to stay together without any fresh envisioning. In addition there were some from both churches who found the thought of a new vision exciting. With so much divergence, many were bound to feel disappointed. Moving on for me was not going to be as easy as it may have sounded.

Although this is all rather painful to recall, it's probably the right point for us to pause and look objectively at my vision-sharing process. In each case I was making over-optimistic assumptions about people's openness to setting out in a new direction. In the first instance I was assuming that London church leaders who had poured so much time and effort into two major capital-based missions within six years would be open to another London-wide initiative. In the second instance I assumed that background information had been shared without taking into account that others might have judged that aspects of it would be better left unsaid. If I compare this with Paul's return to Ephesus, the parallels are certainly not direct but there are a few lessons we can learn.

4. Sharing: Gaining a hearing

Like me, Paul has two audiences to address but in each case he's careful to build on what they already know. He met the congregation at the synagogue (his first audience) a year before when passing through Ephesus and spent time reasoning with them. He then left Aquila and Priscilla behind to back up his words. Now he's back reasoning with them once again, investing three months of his time to build on their scriptural knowledge so as to present Jesus to them as their crucified, risen and ascended Messiah.[47] His vision-sharing shows greater wisdom than mine in that, having gone down a similar route many times before, he's developed a greater ease with simply presenting a case and leaving people to decide. Good vision-sharing will always carry an element of such an understanding.[48]

The group of twelve he comes across on his return (his second audience) is very different. He initially steps in with assumptions about their level of knowledge but is quicker than I was to rethink and start his sharing further back. There is certainly a gap to fill between their knowledge of John's baptism and the understanding that led them to be baptised in the name of Jesus to seal their repentance and new-found faith.[49] I also had a gap to fill in my vision-sharing with the resident church but failed to spot the lack of previously received information in time to prevent damage. I knew them to be a great church full of the Holy Spirit with a vision for the future, but they'd missed out on the opportunity to respond to information agreed behind the scenes on their behalf. This left a hole that was never properly filled.

The thing that apparently caused the most below-the-radar disturbance was my approach to church discipline. I have a strong

---

47. Acts 19:8.
48. Acts 17:2-3; 18:19-21.
49. Acts 19:1-7.

preference for correcting people in private rather than in public, and I guess that left people confused as to how to deal with me. There was a desire on the part of some to reprimand me in public, and as this was mooted behind the scenes, people began withholding their tithes. Old style met new style when my predecessor preached on sounding the alarm, and old style triumphed over new. Of course, I can understand it all now and can see that if more had been said openly, by me about my future vision and by others about more recent voting arrangements, my actions may not have been (or seemed) so jarring. Nonetheless, when my proposal for a church plant was announced, no one was in any doubt as to what kind of church that plant might be.

After such a setback it was tempting to feel the shame of my mistakes and to hold back, but I had to take myself in hand. There were people who were keen to join me in fulfilling a wider vision and they needed to be respected. But planting afresh nearby did have its problems, not least as at the time 'nearby' church plants were not permitted by my newly acquired denomination. A bigger challenge would be to create from the outset a significant but gracious distinctiveness to rule out the possibility of it being seen as just a split over personalities. The testimony we had created by coming together was already in jeopardy without adding such an accusation into the mix.

I could end this chapter with a section on the right way to share vision, but I think I've said enough about Paul's approach for you to learn from my mistakes. Although my first attempt at creating an Ephesus-style church had fallen flat, I was grateful for everyone's sake to see things still moving forward. Although those from the attempted merger who joined us to plant afresh numbered about the same as came from my original church, they were not the same people. The age profile of our original church was far younger than that of the church with which we'd spent a year seeking to merge, and in that year I'd deliberately brought the majority of the resident church's youth group into the mainstream of church life. I actually had no option, as many of them were the same age as those I'd been used to working with as leaders. Perhaps it was this that prompted many in their twenties to come with us, including one whom I thought could be the looked-for Silas.

But positives aside, I found it painful that some likened me to the Pied Piper who played his tune and spirited away the youth. It certainly wasn't an easy legacy to leave behind, especially when coupling it with the picture of the overwound clock. However, much to the credit of the resident church's co-pastor and his wife, who had not only served with my predecessor and me but had taken on the leadership of the resident church when I left, a significant number of the young people who stayed went on to serve as full-time Christian leaders. Some served overseas but one now very successfully leads the church we moved on from. I don't offer the following statement as an excuse, but it really is good to know that... 'God is a great repairer'.

Let's catch our breath before we move on from vision-sharing to launching.

Question:

Why are openness and diplomacy so important in vision-sharing?

5. Launching: *The blaze and the blast*

Although the two London-wide missions were held just a few years apart, there were some marked differences. On the surface these could have been dismissed by saying the second had access to better equipment, greater finance and greater experience. But the differences actually went deeper than that, striking at the root of the way many of us had been raised to think. For the first mission it seemed that, behind the high-quality presentation, we had a 'we'll get by on as little as we can' mindset, and we did incredibly well mobilising on that basis. For the second we seemed to shift to 'we'll make sure we have everything we need'. It wasn't a case of professionalism for professionalism's sake, it was all about effectiveness and efficiency. Both approaches, 'bring what you can, no matter how broken' and 'we'll go for the best, then make it available to others', are equally valid illustrations of the gospel. God receives us as we are but then gives us to the world as his best.

For me, in going forward there was something appealing about seeking to present the world with the best. It was a strategic decision and had its risks. It had the potential for opening the door to elitism, suggesting that everyone who joined had to arrive already formed into what God wanted them to be. If not, they'd be expected to hit that goal soon after arriving. It might be worth keeping this in mind as you evaluate our progress over the coming chapters. Working with such a highly aspirational vision can have its downsides as well as its advantages.

In many ways, as we started afresh church-wise, we felt we had already ticked a number of the preliminary boxes for Paul's Ephesus strategy. Experiencing two capital-wide missions had provided an overview of London that matched the opportunity Aquila and Priscilla had when Paul left them in Ephesus while completing his second missionary journey and starting his third. They undoubtedly used their waiting time to assess the spiritual forces at play in the region and to identify the practical opportunities on offer. But they also, of course, set a great example for the soon-to-emerge Ephesian church by giving away their first convert.[50]

As we started out, we also had to let go of a lot of people who'd have been useful to us. Paul eventually started in Ephesus with a group of twelve, plus Aquila and Priscilla, Timothy and his fellow team members, and an unknown number of believing Jews who were keen to follow him after his further three months teaching in the synagogue. We found that once the dust had settled we had a group of 120. We saw this as enough to head straight for our version of Paul's 'School of Tyrannus'.[51] It was our moment to implement our conviction that the word of God could spread to transform a whole region.[52] We set out a few basic principles. One was a commitment to presenting the best, another was a decision to resist any cynicism, such as a 'nothing much grows in the suburbs' mentality. Psalm 24:2 was the basis of the sermon on our first Sunday. If God established the earth on a flood,[53] we certainly weren't going to begin our new church on just a trickle of enthusiasm. We went for high expectations from day one.

---

50. Acts 18:27.
51. Acts 19:9.
52. Acts 19:10.
53. Psalm 24:1-2 KJV.

5. Launching: The blaze and the blast

I think Paul must have had high expectations too as he prepared to hold his first teaching and discussion session in the real School of Tyrannus. For one thing, he definitely wasn't thinking of it as a short-term commitment. He may still have seen Antioch as his base, and it had served him well while he'd been travelling. It had provided stability when local pressure, or the nature of his calling, had seen him moving on quickly from churches he'd been planting. But in Corinth God had shown him that staying longer can have benefits,[54] and he'd returned to Ephesus with every intention of putting down roots and making a major investment. We see him embracing his teaching centre as a gift from God for reaching the province. His excitement would have been infectious. Let's place ourselves in Ephesus as part of his team.

None of us can be in any doubt about his intentions. He's deliberately hired a building that's already known as a public lecture hall. He's obviously keen to reach as many people as possible, choosing times for his sessions that allow local residents to gather. It seems that he's also hoping that people from around the region will come and stay for extended visits. He's excited as he prepares to receive his initial guests, and seems to feel relieved that he's no longer restricted by the ceremonial expectations of the synagogue, or by some of its congregation's negative reactions.[55] Even so, there are some things he'll certainly decide to bring with him. The public reading of Scripture will be one of them.[56] Reading, reasoning and explaining are, as ever, bound to be at the centre of his plan.[57] What is less synagogue-centred, though, is his habit of allowing people to bring a hymn or personal contribution. He encouraged this when

---

54. Acts 18:9-11.
55. Acts 19:9.
56. 1 Timothy 4:13.
57. Acts 17:2-3.

establishing the church in Corinth,[58] and here in Ephesus he'll be raising a church as well as creating a teaching centre. There's clearly a need for a seismic shift in the worship focus throughout the whole of Asia. Aquila and Priscilla are constantly reminding us that there are far more people in Asia committed to worshipping Artemis than would ever have worshipped alongside them in the synagogue. We are going to have to stand firm with him on his conviction that sound teaching from Scripture can change this. The worship of Artemis is clearly affecting trade and everything else, from personal income to civic life.[59] Maybe he'll end his first teaching and discussion session with a hymn, trusting that one day it will be God who receives worship from across the province.

All these thoughts were in our minds too as we set up our new church. The initial home for our 'School of Tyrannus' was a brand-new Methodist church built on a site that had already gained our attention. Amazingly, as soon as the Methodist minister knew we were about to be homeless, he offered us his pristine new building, setting aside the main auditorium for us on Sunday afternoons and any weeknights we might need. It was a tremendous privilege and a huge encouragement. The building carried all the marks of excellence we aspired to and we hadn't even had to ask.

We put their church premises to use for our Sunday services and weekly prayer meetings straight away. At first people didn't know where to find us, but we soon changed that by holding our first teaching week just fifty days after we started. Being keen to maintain strong relations with local churches, we spread invitations as widely as possible. Four weeks after the teaching week a local Baptist church offered us its premises for our first baptisms.

---

58. 1 Corinthians 14:26.
59. Acts 19:19-27.

5. Launching: The blaze and the blast

During that initial August and September, we not only held a children's outreach in a local park but organised and led the local March for Jesus. One of the elders of the church we'd just left, who'd triggered the attempted merger eighteen months earlier, was very gracious in encouraging us to hold on to Genesis 13:14-5. Here, God speaks to Abram after he's released the best land to his nephew Lot, saying, 'Look around from where you are, to the north and south, to the east and west. All the land you see I will give you.' It was a bold promise, yet in those early months we really did seem to be experiencing exceptional favour.

Although the Methodist church was a great venue it wasn't in the town centre. It worked brilliantly as a temporary solution but we could see that our vision would benefit from having a more central location. Ideally we wanted to be as close to the railway station as we were during the year we were sharing. We also thought a location near the High Street would be great as we were already holding regular praise sessions in the pedestrianised area as a way of engaging with the shoppers. Then two things happened in quick succession. The first was that a UK-based Christian book distribution company, for which I was a board member, was looking to set up a national chain of bookshops and wanted the one in our town centre to be its flagship store. I attended meetings to help them look at leasehold premises in and around the newly built shopping mall. The only building that seemed right was between the new shopping mall and the station. It had a basement as large as the building we had recently shared and an equally large suite of separately-leased offices above the retail area. We agreed on a joint venture. The bookshop would take the retail area and we'd take a sublease on the basement while keeping an eye on future space becoming available on the upper floor. We knew refurbishment would take months and stretch our faith financially, but we saw the stretching as no bad thing, and it brought us a step nearer to securing the more public profile we were thinking would be useful. That was the first thing. Something then happened that lifted our public profile even higher than the dizzy peaks of our aspirations.

The new town centre development included a leisure centre. For some reason it was also designed to include a performance suite with lighting rigs and a seating capacity of several hundred, facilitated by pull-out tiered seating. We asked for a guided tour while it was still under construction and delighted the owners by making an offer straightaway to book the performance suite for every Sunday afternoon and evening. The whole complex was so interconnected that the space we were to hire had a viewing gallery that all but led on from the swimming pool, and there were other rooms we could use for our children's sessions. There was so much to take in, and it was all brand new. Our new basement premises and the leisure centre were only a few minutes' walk apart and both had lifts. As the leisure centre's lift was accessible from its car park, transporting equipment between the two locations was going to be relatively easy.

All in all, premises-wise things seemed to be flowing in a direction that fitted well with our strong teaching emphasis. We had secured a very public venue in which to present God's word and a space for ensuring that our prayer-base was equally strong. Even before our basement was fitted out with its carefully-planned sports hall, lounge, studio, kitchen and offices, it became our prayer centre. We made sure we could pray in the midst of the building work. Prayer was so central, especially to our London vision, that I'll shortly devote a whole chapter to it, but I can't move on from describing our launch year without mentioning how we prioritised our members serving overseas. Within our first twelve months we made two visits

5. Launching: The blaze and the blast

to Pakistan and the Emirates – once I went on my own and once with my young co-leader. Six months later we were in Malaysia.

I have called this chapter 'the blast and the blaze' because of the account in Judges where Gideon claims back the land from the Midianites. In the prayer chapter I'll explain why this Bible passage became important for us. Right now I'm turning to it because so far I may have given the impression that launching for us was all about making as much noise as possible. The Judges' account certainly contains a mighty trumpet blast but there is far more to it than that.

The Midianites are thick on the ground. They've arrived yet again with their allies and livestock, camping on the crops and spoiling the land. Gideon, who's shown some spirit by threshing grain in a winepress, as if saying defiantly, 'Why should the Midianites have all the harvest?' overcomes his nerves and rallies an army of 32,000. But God has him split this down until he has released all but a watchful 300. On the night chosen for action, as 10pm approaches, he positions his 300 men in three groups on the hills around the valley where the Midianites are camped. None of the 300 has a sword, but they each have a trumpet in their right hand and a burning torch covered by a jar in their left. At Gideon's signal they break the jars, shine the light, blow the trumpets and shout, 'A sword for the Lord and for Gideon.' They then hold their ground, torches still blazing, while the Midianites flee in confusion, eventually being pursued by, among others, some of the warriors who were earlier sent home.[60]

I want you to see that while boldness was the key to the blast, brokenness was the key to the blaze. I can only hope, in retrospect, that as we started afresh, the humility this brokenness implies was present alongside our trumpet blast. If there had been no brokenness,

---

60. Judges 6:11 – 7:25.

there would have been no blazing light. I trust that if you come to a point when you think it appropriate to launch (or relaunch) your project, or maybe even to announce your assignment, you'll ensure that there's the humility of brokenness facilitating a blaze as well a blast.

Question:

What would you see as the appropriate hallmarks of a good launch for a new initiative?

Developing

Expanding — Partnering — Engaging — Persisting — Coordinating

6. Expanding: *Broadening the appeal*

There is a story (probably fabricated) that is told about a local radio station that scheduled a phone-in programme on apathy. The presenter was well set with music tracks to play in between callers. In the end he played every track he had and then had to select some more. He sat through the whole programme without receiving a single call. Now, just as phone-in programmes need callers, strategic initiatives need participants, people who buy into the vision and are so excited by it they recruit others. And if it's apathy that deters, it's energy that attracts. We were aiming for energy in abundance and after we've once again given some thought to Paul, we'll explore how that works.

If you want the word of God to go throughout a region, you need people. Visionaries love to quote the King James version of Proverbs 29:18, 'Where there is no vision, the people perish.' But Paul as a strategist would have known the reverse to be equally true, 'Where there are no people, the vision perishes.' He did not expect the word to waft on the wind, as the early nineteenth-century writer of the missionary hymn 'From Greenland's icy mountains' implied.[61] He knew he needed people to carry the word to every community, and who better to do that than people from those communities. As Jesus had done before him, he needed to 'gather' in order to 'send'. The School of Tyrannus had to become a focal point for visitors as well as for locals. His ministry in Ephesus had to be attractive. He needed

---

61. 'Waft, waft, ye winds, His story, and you, ye waters, roll, till, like a sea of glory, it spreads from pole to pole.' Reginald Heber, 'From Greenland's icy mountains', 3rd verse (public domain, 1819).

to play to his God-given strengths. He could reason and teach, and had the ability to mobilise. If God would graciously, constantly and consistently empower the gifts he carried, there could be a breakthrough.

He knew it would take humility. His grasp of Israel's history shows him that relying on gifts rather than their Giver can turn the whole exercise into nothing more than an empty show. He's glad he's chosen to be called Paul.[62] Saul had too many associations with kingly aggrandisement and insecure self-centredness.[63] Recalling his name-change on Cyprus focuses his thinking as he helps prepare the room for yet another daily teaching session.[64] Everyone knows the school is not about him. It's one hundred per cent about Jesus, crucified, resurrected and reigning as Lord. He loves sharing with the people rather than lecturing them. It really is a teaching centre, encouraging people to discuss and think for themselves. There's nothing dictatorial about it. And even though it might be called a school, reflecting the building it meets in, he isn't looking to be labelled as the 'headmaster' or to have a private office with 'Principal' on the door. He's happy to be simply 'Paul the teacher', available to all, along with the rest of his team, creating a learning community with a relational atmosphere where everyone can be there for everyone else. He breaks off his musing to look across the room to Timothy and his other team members as they work with Priscilla and Aquila to straighten the benches. That glance is enough to assure him that the vision won't fail. It'll start with a centre and become a province-wide movement.

---

62. Derived from the Latin for 'small'.
63. 1 Samuel 15:12,17-26.
64. Luke records the name change as having taken place in the proconsul's house on Cyprus (Acts 13:9).

6. Expanding: Broadening the appeal

What could he have seen in that presumed moment that may have made him so sure? I think it would have been two things: understanding and commitment, and he'd have recognised they came in that order. Expansion always involves people, but at the heart of an expansion programme, the people who are needed to get things going have to have a really clear understanding of the vision and a strong commitment to its fulfilment. These come through time spent with the vision-sharer. On his way back to Ephesus he'd travelled through Cilicia, Galatia and Phrygia. Some of those across the room had travelled with him, providing ample opportunity for some strong bonding.[65] But to Paul, these young team members are certainly more than travelling companions. They're friends and fellow workers he's recruited and is training along the way. He's keen that those working alongside him understand not only his words but his thinking too. He's happy to be completely transparent so they can grow to anticipate his responses and predict his moves. Timothy has certainly reached that point.[66] He's been with Paul in Macedonia and Corinth, and wasn't chosen lightly. Now, after a few years of being side-by-side and crossing many miles together, they've built a genuine father and son relationship. These young men alone would be sufficient to make his vision work. But then he also has Aquila and Priscilla whom he's lived and worked with in Corinth. They are a couple who completely understand his strategy. None of them has made a blind commitment to him and his vision, any more than he has to them and to their visions. The strong understanding between them undergirds everything. There's absolutely no doubt that they'll all be pulling together and taking things in the same direction.

---

65. Travelling as part of a team seems to have been a favoured approach (Acts 20:4).
66. 1 Corinthians 4:17.

Having a core team like this is important. Even so, if there's really going to be an expansion, it's not possible to be open just to the few and closed to the many. Of course there'll be different levels of relationship. That was true even for those around Jesus, but he made even the youngest person in a crowd feel valued and appreciated. Back in south-east London we were choosing the people to whom we would give responsibility. We trod carefully as our aim was to let everyone see we trusted them by supporting their leadership without ever overriding them or undermining them. Confidence along these lines is important. We didn't have Paul's ministry to draw people in our direction, but we did share a passion for changing our borough and were praying together fervently to see the nation's capital transformed.

What we lacked in terms of skills we definitely could make up for in energy. We could study to teach and then bring in guest speakers to make up our shortfall. We could go out into the streets and reach into local housing areas. We could hold one-off events in public halls around London, and continue to organise programmes in parks, not just for children but for teenagers and young adults too. In addition, we could use our newly acquired and soon-to-be-refurbished basement in the heart of town as a base for reaching businesses and shoppers. We had plenty of outlets and opportunities for our energy. There were indications, though, that it would be in our worship that our energy would become particularly evident. It seemed that people, young and old, whether previously worshippers or not, had a hunger to worship in a liberated way and we were meeting the need.

I'd already witnessed my young co-leader's worship-leading gift when I was pastoring the merging churches but in our new environment it came more strongly to the fore. He led with energy and mobilised everyone with enthusiasm. We had good musicians, yet he managed to avoid any sense of performance. Standing still to watch and listen never felt like an option. The momentum came from everyone singing, moving and expressing themselves as part of a communal vibrancy. We made sure the words we sang were inspiring, bursting with hope and affirmation while at the same time being full of adoration and gratitude. We looked globally for suitable songs, drawing from the States and Australia, but eventually began to write and record our own.

As a teaching centre, seeing people mature was part of our plan and we had to make sure that in growing together, we kept our freshness. Having a constant inflow of new people was part of the answer, but it also depended on the new arrivals being made new and sharing their enthusiasm for their new-found faith. The invitation for everyone to meet Jesus as their crucified and risen Saviour and Lord had to be unmissable. Our aim was transformation, not assimilation. We particularly watched our use of 'could' and 'should'. We didn't teach 'this is who you should be in Christ'. We taught 'this is who you can be in Christ'. Our style may not have been totally otherworldly, far from it, but, in our desire to present relevantly, we were still uncompromisingly offering a world that was fundamentally different, a world that is full of God's light, life and love. And we were prepared to do this on the streets and in the parks, welcoming all the exposure that public spaces afford.

I know that as you read this you'll realise that different types of projects and initiatives will need to expand in different ways, but however you choose to expand, avoid thinking of it as simply building a support base. Our expansion was not about building a support base so much as getting on with the work we were called to do. Reaching out into the streets, parks and local communities to meet people and to share God's word with them directly was the 'intended end', not just a means towards it. This had to be at the front of our minds, whether we were holding sessions of public praise on local high streets, talking to young people who were out on the streets in large numbers on Friday and Saturday nights, putting on well-publicised youth concerts in local parks or holding tent campaigns in the middle of densely packed communities.

We were determined not to hold back, not just putting leaflets through people's doors but coming up with ways to have audio recordings delivered to every house.[67] Our aim was to have the widest possible mobilisation. We never had a separate evangelism team or a separate events team. Everyone who could participate did participate, and my co-leader and I set the pace, delegating responsibility where we could but being present to support and serve everyone to whom we gave responsibility. As much as possible we wanted this to feel like a celebration of the whole church agenda being owned by all with everyone doing everything.

While we were working as a young and growing church in our own London borough, we were also thinking London-wide. I was still involved in organising the London Leaders' Prayer Gatherings with CARE and the Evangelical Alliance but I hadn't lost my desire to win people over to a vision for transforming London as a whole. I'd been invited to an event in Surrey to hear Ray McCauley, a church leader from South Africa who was credited with influencing his government in the closing days of apartheid. I was impressed and we started working as a church to invite Ray to London for what we decided to call a Faith for London Conference. It was to be a two-day event at Wembley Conference Centre. Ray's contribution

---

67. This was at a time when we discovered the postal service would deliver cassette recordings to every house within certain postcodes.

6. Expanding: Broadening the appeal

was inspiring, even if the meeting that my co-leader and I had with him the day before was a little unsettling. He shared the thought of the Church in a city transforming not just the city but the nation. Fortunately, we had enough wisdom to think step-by-step and hold to our more limited Ephesus blueprint. If we hadn't, we may well have ended up trying to fly while we were still learning to run. Paul's vision had been 'Ephesus for Asia'; sufficient for us, at that stage at least, to hold on to 'south-east London for the capital'.

We repeated the Faith for London conference later in the year with other guest speakers who reflected some growing partnerships. Partnerships for us were becoming an essential part of our vision and marked a particular mindset that can be important when thinking about expanding. It's 'partnership' that we'll be considering next.

Question:

How much do you agree with the statement that 'without people a vision will perish', and how much do you think that thought should stand alongside the original Proverbs 29:18 statement?

7. Partnering: *Finding fellow travellers*

We were not only travelling fast but we were planning to travel far. It was a strategy that was bound to put pressure on the East African proverb, 'If you want to travel fast, travel alone. If you want to travel far, travel together.' 'Fast alone' had no appeal for us, and 'far together' would only work if our fellow travellers were prepared to keep moving at our speed. Strangely enough, when I was preaching on Jacob's life at a conference in East Africa I was reassured to discover that the believers there were not the least bit bound by the proverb's implication that together means slower. As I explained that the limping Jacob reduced his pace for the sake of the young in his family and flock,[68] I thought I'd ask the question, 'How many of you would keep up if your pastor moved faster?' To the amazement of the many church leaders who were there, everyone indicated they'd gladly try. As I visited year-after-year I could see that many of them had really meant it.

Paul had no problem working with leaders raised by others. He and Barnabas were together on their first missionary trip to Cyprus and Galatia. Not only was Barnabas raised in the church in Jerusalem but so was John Mark who was with them at the outset. On his second trip from Antioch he had Silas with him, taking on Timothy in Lystra and Luke in Troas. Silas was also raised in the church in Jerusalem.[69] As we planned our way forward, we took heart from this. We could already see that some of the expertise we

---

68. Genesis 33:13.
69. Acts 15:40 – 16:3a. Note Luke's use of 'we' in Acts 16:10.

needed would have to come from those who'd been travelling similar roads and could bring their experience with them. The invitation they received must have sounded daunting. In effect we said, 'We're intending to travel far and fast, are you interested in joining us?'

We don't know what specific gifts Timothy, Aquila, Priscilla, Erastus, Gaius and Aristarchus brought to Paul's Ephesus team, but as we were thinking of possible invitations, church ministers around us were seeking to create leadership teams that represented all five of the ministry gifts listed in Ephesians 4:11. It was as if they were convinced that Paul would never have referred to apostles, prophets, evangelists, pastors and teachers when writing his follow-up letter to the Ephesians from Rome if he hadn't previously made sure of that balance when starting out in Asia. Of course, it's clear from his letter that he would have wanted everyone attending the School of Tyrannus to be able to teach, to think pastorally, to act evangelistically, to engage prophetically and to function apostolically. He was clearly more interested in creating generalists than raising specialists. It's also clear, though, that he knew time would show that every individual would be more gifted in some areas than in others. That's how God ensures we complement each other rather than end up all being totally self-sufficient.[70]

We were confident that guest speakers could help us with this breadth of ministry-equipping, but we knew we needed people on our team who could provide us with well-honed administrative, organisational and technical skills. We prayed that the right people would cross our paths. We needed four in particular, and each has their own story to tell. Generally in this book I'm not giving names

---

70. Ephesians 4:7-16.

7. Partnering: Finding fellow travellers

but in this chapter some of the stories are already so far into the public domain that it would seem silly to try to cover up.

The first story I'll tell leads on from our two Faith for London conferences. Many of the attendees were either would-be African church planters or young Caribbean leaders with aspirations beyond their denominations. All were thinking of launching out afresh with a view to impacting the capital. We announced a pastors' lunch between the sessions and many of the attendees came. The informal lunch proved such a fertile time for information-sharing that there was a request that we should host something similar every other month. Our basement centre was near completion so we would have the space if we could find a coordinator. A young Nigerian volunteered and we brought him onto our team as an associate minister. He did an incredible job in setting everything up and securing a regular attendance. The Ministers' Fellowship has run ever since and led to some incredible breakthroughs, which will get a mention in chapter 13 and form the basis of the next book in this series. Many who went on to lead powerful, high-profile churches were helped in the early days of their ministry by the Ministers' Fellowship.

The second story arises from my conviction that behind every successful church there is an incredibly effective church administrator. Such administrators are never difficult to spot but are notoriously hard to recruit as they're always more than fully employed. It looked impossible, but since the Graham mission one of the central London churches that had approached me to consider a staff appointment had continued to book me for their lunchtime services for those working in the square mile which officially constitutes the City of London. The church had a superb administrator and having prayed and prayed, I took my courage in both hands and asked if a move might be on her mind. It seemed a ridiculous thing to ask, but what I thought would be just a slight possibility proved to be more on target than I could ever have imagined. A house move in our direction was soon underway and we were blessed with a superb, experienced administrator who seemed to take even our wildest plans in her stride.

Story number three also relates back to the Graham mission. Some areas of London had too few participating churches to handle the numbers who responded to the gospel. We worked hard to put people into discovery groups and toyed with the idea of waiting lists. That, though, would have delayed some people's post-mission engagement until the autumn. A friend of mine then had a novel idea. Why not send them a video that covers all the discovery group content? I loved the idea and suggested to the mission staff that they ask Billy Graham himself to record it. To everyone's amazement he agreed. It was then I discovered how far the UK Christian world was lagging behind the media scene. Although we found a good Christian film producer, the choice was virtually non-existent. There were plenty of 'want-to-be's and hardly any 'can-do's. I was shocked at the lack of competence and desperately wanted to set new standards of excellence that would shake the complacency I was meeting all around me.

With this disappointment fresh in my mind, I learnt that one of our UK mainstream TV channels was keen to put out Christian stories. I decided to find out more by speaking to the leader of a project that had already been filmed. I found out that having to go outside the Christian world to find competence was compromising spiritual sensitivity. The stories were great but the crew had no idea how to respect the lives of those involved. I thought we should set up a production house to make documentaries for mainstream TV

7. Partnering: Finding fellow travellers

and I started praying that God would speak to someone in the States to come and run it for us. Little did I know that God had already spoken a directional word to an Englishman who had gone to the States as a sound engineer. He'd switched his attention to television while out there, buying his own US standard equipment and getting his training around local TV stations. The guiding word someone gave him was that 'God wants you to go back to the UK to take the airwaves for Christ'. I guess that after that the link-up was inevitable. Howard Conder joined us and we found a temporary studio while a new one was being built in our basement premises. The basement turned out to be the perfect place for filming. There were no variations in natural light and no risk of sound pollution.

We needed and prayed for one but gained three. Rory and Wendy Alec arrived from South Africa and joined us soon afterwards. Wendy would help with scriptwriting and Rory would assist in developing a media department. We required equipment and God opened the way for us to get the camera equipment that had been used in filming an award-winning film. A camera crew was next on the list and we decided to train our own by filming our Sunday services. We had no shortage of volunteers. In my mind it was all practice for the documentaries, but Rory had bolder ideas. He asked permission to offer what we'd filmed to a TV company and before we knew it we were providing the Sunday service on a black entertainment channel.

So on to story number four, and this one is pretty obvious given our Ephesian vision. If we were reproducing the School of Tyrannus, we needed to do more about the 'daily teaching' referred to in Acts 19:9, yet we didn't want something daily to be any less energetic than our times together Sunday by Sunday. Anyone visiting our public services in the leisure centre would have been impacted by the teaching as well as the worship. In fact everything in our gatherings was seen as worship and the preaching was presented with the same energy and enthusiasm as our singing. We weren't in the business of holding back. We taught systematically, often covering a theme across six weeks with my co-leader and me sharing the teaching.

There was one Sunday when the company running the leisure centre wanted some photographs to publicise the availability of their performance suite so they sent in a team of photographers. They set up their cameras on stands at the back of the tiered seating, pointing down across all the heads to capture the stage and the lighting rigs. I expected them to leave soon after we began but they just stood there for ages without taking a shot. Later one of the photographers came to visit me in my basement office, saying they were so overwhelmed that at first they thought that even taking shots might disturb what they sensed was a highly charged atmosphere. In the end, though, they changed their minds and wanted to capture as much of the atmosphere as they could. More importantly, the photographer who came to see me asked if he could demonstrate his Christian commitment by being baptised. His account reinforced our thoughts about dynamism and, if I had time, I'd take you to our quarterly teaching weeks too. But it's daily teaching we're thinking about here and it's already proving to be a story with a number of twists and turns. So here's one final twist before I share the outcome.

We were beginning to think that a London-wide vision could do with a central London focus as well as a south-east London one. Zechariah 2:4-5 had been inspiring us: "'Jerusalem will be a city without walls... And I myself will be a wall of fire around it,' declares the Lord, "and I will be its glory within." We weren't thinking of London as Jerusalem but we were interested in the wall of fire and the glory within. Mobilising churches to collaborate and pray could

7. Partnering: Finding fellow travellers

contribute to God's wall of fire, and maybe a central London, full-time Bible college, open to all, could help to reveal the glory within. We were encouraged in this by a couple who were leading London-wide prayer conferences. The husband had been involved with fire-fighting in North America and spoke of a film he'd seen giving an aerial view of a circle of fire where the flames bent inwards until they touched and the fire burnt out. The scientific explanation was that the bending resulted from oxygen depletion, but in applying the picture to churches, it was a bending in humility and unity that came to mind. So what kind of college could we put in the centre to reflect God's glory and encourage those flames to bend? Well, a college bringing in a wide range of lecturers teaching God's word would speak of both unity and God's glory, and if it operated from Monday to Friday, it would pretty much give us our daily schedule. Incredibly we found the right person to help us deliver exactly this.

Peter Rowe and I are about the same age. He has a doctorate in practical theology and had been running a Bible college for a large church in Australia before returning to the UK to plant a London congregation. A brief conversation revealed that not only was his passion for running a college still active but that he'd written all the course notes and had the contacts for a viable faculty. It took very little persuading to bring him onto our team and we set about obtaining the premises, administrative team and recruitment programme to make it all happen. Our plan was coming together well. We now had the media, the college, the administration and the Ministers' Fellowship up and running and beginning to interconnect. There was, however, one more vital piece of partnership to bring into play.

During the year that I was leading the two churches, I heard there had been a prophecy circulating around the various Christian Business Men's Fellowship meetings that London was about to be picked up by its four corners. When I was told this, the map of London came back to mind and I started thinking about how it might work if we could partner with three key churches that could complement our city-resourcing vision. We would be in the south working with churches that held similar visions for London in the west, east and north. In Paul's day the Roman province of Asia may have been ten times the size of London within the M25, but the density of London's population still made it a massive challenge. Partnership was essential and 2,000 years of church history meant that we were never going to be lone pioneers. Whereas Paul's plan for Asia would lead to planting churches throughout the region, London already had thousands of active churches. Our aim would be to have a highly motivated resource centre in each quadrant of London, encouraging as many churches as possible to think in terms of community transformation. We were sure God was prompting others to think along similar lines.

Kensington Temple was an obvious choice for a western partner. It was well-established, had an events agenda and a very successful Bible college. It was also well-networked, even beyond its denominational affiliation. Colin Dye, its minister, agreed to speak at one of our Faith for London conferences, and his message on being watchmen on the walls led to him thinking of us as the gatekeepers of the south gate. This gateway label greatly influenced our thinking and praying, as will become clear in the chapter after next. But it also led to us praying for an east gate and north gate, and our eastward thoughts began to focus on a newly planted church in Hackney where Matthew Ashimolowo, its pastor, was proving not only to be a real visionary but a very determined implementer and innovator. My co-leader and I made a point of being present at the opening of Kingsway's (KICC's) first owned Hackney premises, completely unaware of what God was about to do.

Question:

How important is it to have fellow travellers when seeking to implement a vision?

8. Engaging: *Walking together*

Even before we began pressing forward on multiple fronts, I was haunted by a deep and authoritative voice. It was a throwback to a post-mission reception for key workers put on by the Graham organisation. I was in conversation with a missionary from the Caribbean who was highly respected for the depth of his experience. He'd been heading up the minority ethnic engagement for the mission and I was sharing with him my regret at having been unable to fully mobilise his constituency. I'm sure his response must have been heard by everyone present as it boomed across the room, but I, being the intended recipient, was probably the only one to be left with it ringing in my ears: 'You will never get the black churches involved in your white agenda until you get involved in theirs.' I'd always seen that helping people fulfil their God-given agendas was something I was called to do. This was different, though. It wasn't about coming alongside to shape an initiative, it was about supporting what was entirely someone else's enterprise.

I was still working with the Evangelical Alliance to set up a London-wide prayer initiative when an invitation came to attend a meeting being hosted by the American Pentecostal evangelist Morris Cerullo. He was planning to hold a Mission to London just two years after the Graham one had concluded. I went to the meeting thinking that this was surely going to be too much, too soon, but I was impressed by the ethnic diversity of the leaders present. I sat there listening to the event coordinator, and my overwhelming emotion was one of relief: 'If this goes ahead, I won't have to be involved.' But as I listened I became concerned that things I'd come to see as key elements of a mission were being given little attention. In the end my concern got the better of me and I spoke to the event coordinator, mentioning my previous mission roles and allowing him to take my name and details. Evidently he left the meeting, contacted Morris Cerullo in the States and said that the mission had its first member of a council of reference.

The next meeting I attended was no longer so ethnically diverse. Those who were well known to me were no longer there. The questions they'd asked about Cerullo's style and healing emphasis obviously still troubled them. Interestingly this hadn't affected the overall numbers. Word had obviously spread among those who'd attended Cerullo's earlier London-based rallies. Looking around, I could see that I was surrounded by people who were used to a very different way of doing things. I realised I'd stumbled on the very churches and leaders whose agendas I'd been told I needed to engage with.

I continued on the council of reference, and for the first year's event at Earls Court the council was just my co-leader and me. But I was encouraged when I was asked if I could bring the leaders of KT and KICC alongside us for year two. By the time we reached year three, there was talk among the Cerullo team of the mission being handed over to London leaders, and it was clear that those forming the council of reference were the leaders in mind. My hopes of seeing London being picked up by the four corners seemed to be coming into place. I was prayerfully asking God for a similarly minded pick-up point in the north.

But what was said to me by my Caribbean friend included the word 'until'. Having my passions and plans described as 'my white agenda' was fair comment. Prejudice and presumptions of entitlement definitely need to be called out. As one-time missionary candidates, Marion and I had to examine ourselves in preparing to go to Africa,[71] and I still feel so strongly about prejudice and presumption that I'm open to being challenged again and again to make sure I stay free from unconscious bias. Even so, it was the little word 'until' that humbled me. Mutual engagement for mutual benefit was not being ruled out.

Now I've often pointed out that the Bible doesn't say 'give *so that* it shall be given to you'.[72] For me, 'giving to get' is not really giving at all. I certainly was way past any thought of engaging with other people's agendas to get them to engage with mine. But I couldn't deny that something was happening. It was undeniable that the more I gave myself to support other people's plans, the more readily they supported mine. This had to be God, and I was loving the way he was doing it. I was making friends with people and the people I befriended were coming alongside me as friends in return. With this in mind, I thought it would be good for our Sunday services to better reflect London's diversity. One Sunday, when our second service at the leisure centre was not particularly full, I asked anyone who had at least one non-white grandparent to come down from the tiered seating and stand with me at the front to pray. There were only a few, but it was a moving moment and also a very clear declaration of intent. It caught the heart of the church and helped to draw everyone together in anticipation of the change that followed.

The next step in my thinking was prompted by the discovery that the kind of speakers that were motivating my non-white colleagues were not British Bible teachers but American motivational speakers, people who could hold sway through their books, their conferences

---

71. You can read about this in *Unstoppable Church*, the first book in this series.
72. See Luke 6:38.

and their recorded messages. I'd already met such preferences on overseas trips and had returned thinking that maybe we needed to challenge any underlying arrogance in our widespread UK presumptions. The desire to do so was all the stronger now that I knew there was a stream of affection in the UK for such American speakers. We decided to offer them a platform to see if we could establish an area of common ground.

A good starting point seemed to be to host American church leaders who'd worked with UK publishers to have their books printed for a British market. Their covers had become more muted and their spelling and punctuation had been edited accordingly. Benny Hinn had published *Good Morning, Holy Spirit* and Larry Lea had published *Learning the Joy of Prayer*,[73] and in the minds of UK readers anglicising their books must have anglicised their writers. We hosted Benny Hinn at the Wembley Arena and Larry Lea at the Fairfield Halls, Croydon. Both meetings were well attended, with the hoped-for ethnic diversity very much in evidence. However, neither of the speakers was as British as some had hoped. We remained undeterred and went on to host others, always believing that the common ground might be just around the corner.

But the hope of finding such shared appreciation was beginning to recede. While the African and Caribbean churches were supporting Cerullo's Mission to London, other churches that were less broadly US-sympathetic were lobbying for Cerullo's membership of the Evangelical Alliance to be removed. I was caught in the middle trying to arbitrate, knowing that more was at stake in terms of inter-church relations than most people realised. It was like living in two different worlds. On one occasion Morris Cerullo said to me, 'I don't

---

73. Benny Hinn, *Good Morning, Holy Spirit* (Milton Keynes: Word Books, 1991). Larry Lea, *Learning the Joy of Prayer* (Bradford: Harvestime, 1989).

suppose you experienced reactions like this when working with Billy Graham.' I had to reply, 'Oh, yes I did. He just had a very different support base.'[74] Anyone who thinks they can gain widespread Church approval simply by choosing whom to support or not to support needs to know that association and dissociation can each attract as much blame as favour. Having said that, though, it was humbling to see how much credibility we as a church were gaining with African and Caribbean churches across London and around the UK. Invitations began to come to us from the church leaders visiting the UK whom we hosted as preachers as the make-up of our own congregation changed. We'd been travelling to support our members overseas but now we were breaking fresh ground visiting our new members' home churches and home countries.[75]

So back to Paul in Ephesus where at times he too must feel as if he's living in two worlds, leading one church while supporting another. The church in Corinth is never far from his mind. A trip across the Aegean Sea, port city to port city, is all it would take to reach him from Achaia, and some do. Sosthenes, the ruler of the synagogue in Corinth who'd been beaten instead of Paul when the Jewish community were protesting about Paul to the proconsul, made the journey.[76] He may have brought with him some concerns shared by his fellow believers in the Corinthian church, and these may have prompted Paul to write to them briefly about the need to walk in purity.[77] But other news begins to reach Paul too: there's a case of incest in the church and believers are taking fellow believers

---

74. I was one of the people asked to deal with the correspondence that came into the office for Billy Graham. It was not all complimentary.
75. Those who've read *Unstoppable Church* will know the significance of this. Africa had come to us and we were now going to Africa. See *Unstoppable Church*, p. 60.
76. Acts 18:12-17; 1 Corinthians 1:1.
77. 1 Corinthians 5:9 – a letter that was not preserved, probably because the teaching was repeated in 1 Corinthians.

to court.[78] Combined gatherings are running the risk of becoming disorderly and some believers are questioning if there's an afterlife.[79] Food offered to idols is also a problem.[80] But the biggest concern is that the church is divided into factions, making it difficult to deal with any issue at all.[81] In the midst of this some members write to him about marriage.[82]

We have no way of knowing who brings the letter. It could have been Stephanas. His household were the first converts in Achaia and he's arrived in Ephesus with Fortunatus and Achaicus, and is proving to be a reliable source of information for Paul.[83] On the other hand it might have been Apollos who's become so concerned about the Corinthian factions that he's made the journey to Ephesus himself.[84] Not only is he relieved to unburden himself to Paul (whom he at last has a chance to work with) but is thrilled to meet up again with Aquila and Priscilla. With at least five prominent people from Corinth around him, Paul certainly has more than one agenda to handle.

How similar were the two churches Paul was having to work with? Probably remarkably so on the surface. They had both been founded by him and his team. Yet there were differences, some because of the way things had developed in Corinth since his departure and some because of the way they were when he was there. Looking back, he knew the Corinthian church to be a very vocal church, where getting people to contribute never seemed to be a problem, but he was aware that they hadn't been ready for the depth of teaching he was now able

---

78. 1 Corinthians 5:1 – 6:6.
79. 1 Corinthians 14:26; 15:12.
80. 1 Corinthians 8:1-13.
81. 1 Corinthians 1:10-12.
82. 1 Corinthians 7:1.
83. 1 Corinthians 16:15-18.
84. 1 Corinthians 16:12.

to deliver daily at the School of Tyrannus.[85] He also knew the church had always been keen to assert its freedoms and express its opinions. He was totally with them in promoting freedom (with some culturally-aware restraints), but could see that opinions were getting out of hand. Both Corinth and Ephesus had meetings in homes, but the fact that all the believers in both places still gathered together (weekly in Corinth and daily in Ephesus) made the rise of factions a surprise. The Corinthian split was heading in four directions. Peter had acquired a following, probably because of respectful comments made by Paul when establishing the church. Others were trying to set up Apollos on a competitive pedestal alongside Paul. Then there were those who wanted to assert their sole allegiance to Christ but were doing so in an arrogant way.[86]

As Paul spends time prayerfully considering how to respond, he drafts a letter which he would like Apollos to take back. As Apollos learns of Paul's reply, he's amazed at his graciousness. Paul could so easily be insisting, 'I'm the founding apostle and everyone owes their allegiance to me,' but he isn't thinking like that at all. He recognises how different gifts can complement each other and there's no selfishness in his thinking. He writes, 'I planted the seed, Apollos watered it, but God has been making it grow.'[87] The rest of the letter is a lesson in wisdom and fatherly care.[88] Paul begins by celebrating the Corinthian believers before addressing all of his concerns and helping reset their course. In the end it's taken by Timothy and some of the team, rather than by Apollos who prefers to delay his return.[89]

---

85. 1 Corinthians 3:1-3.
86. 1 Corinthians 1:10-12.
87. 1 Corinthians 3:5-6.
88. 1 Corinthians 4:15.
89. 1 Corinthians 16:10-12.

The whole letter reminds me of how Elisha solved a problem with a handful of flour when his company of prophets were eating a meal that had something inappropriate sliced into it, and began shouting, 'There is death in the pot!'[90] It was essential support for Corinth, and it all took place while Paul continued to teach daily in the School of Tyrannus and to wrestle with the challenges of Roman Asia.

Back in south London we could see that coming alongside others is important, and that to be an Elisha with a handful of flour might take years of building trust. Even so, 'until' was definitely something to aspire to and in the meantime (to use Paul's metaphor) we could water the seeds of others while planting our own.

Question:

How open would you be to working with people on their agendas rather than just working on your own? What benefits do you see in such an approach, and if you detect any possible problems, what safeguards could you put in place?

---

90. 2 Kings 4:38-41.

9. Persisting: *Pursuing with passion*

Paul's ability to give time to Corinth while working flat out at Ephesus is remarkable, but in his letter to the Corinthians he does give a few insights into what is primarily occupying his time. In correcting their distorted view of apostleship, he spells out his present reality by saying,

> For it seems to me that God has put us apostles on display at the end of the procession, like those condemned to die in the arena. We have been made a spectacle to the whole universe, to angels as well as to human beings.[91]

Everyone in Corinth would have known of the vast amphitheatre in Ephesus. It's still there today and its seating capacity is estimated to be 25,000. It would once have been home to Greek dramas, but Roman entertainment had its gorier side. In Paul's day, fights with animals and armed gladiators were the spectacles that everyone on the high terraces wanted to look down on. In a region dominated by Diana worship, the amphitheatre was the city's main attraction after the Temple. Later in his letter, Paul emphasises the power of resurrection hope by saying, 'If I fought wild beasts in Ephesus with no more than human hopes, what have I gained?'[92] For the Corinthians, the Ephesian amphitheatre would immediately have come to mind. But this needs some further explanation. Eventually,

---
91. 1 Corinthians 4:9.
92. 1 Corinthians 15:32.

once he has travelled on from Ephesus to Macedonia, Paul writes again to the Corinthians telling them how incredibly hard pressed he'd been in Ephesus. This may have made them wonder if his reference to 'beasts' had actually been more than an eye-catching illustration.

> We were under great pressure, far beyond our ability to endure, so that we despaired of life itself. Indeed, we felt we had received the sentence of death. But this happened that we might not rely on ourselves but on God, who raises the dead.[93]

Maybe the fighting was genuine and the beasts he was pitched against were not animals in the arena but spiritual forces dominating the province. This may be why he later wrote to the Ephesians themselves, 'For our struggle is not against flesh and blood, but against the rulers, against the authorities, against the powers of this dark world and against the spiritual forces of evil in the heavenly realms.'[94]

We were concentrating on bringing community transformation by setting up a regional teaching centre, but I was aware of others who were committed to securing regional change through prayer. A small incident had brought this to my attention when the Graham mission was using a much more recently built arena, the 30,000-capacity stadium at Crystal Palace. There were traffic jams nearby because many coaches were trying to deliver attendees at the same time. I was at the hub of preparations one evening when one of our runners came from checking the various pre-meeting gatherings to tell us, with a smile on his face, that all would be solved

---

93. 2 Corinthians 1:8-9.
94. Ephesians 6:12.

9. Persisting: Pursuing with passion

as the intercessors had just taken control of the junction where the hold-ups were at their worst. I smiled too, but that sentence was an introduction to a way of praying that was to become very important to us. It seemed to assume a delegated responsibility based on a confident understanding of God's desired outcome and a boldness to stand with him to see it accomplished in the face of every obstacle. At first there were times when I felt that some of those adopting this approach relied more on their derived authority to defeat the opposition than on the Lord with whom they were standing, but as I travelled more globally I found myself in cultures where people prayed with a passion that might put us to shame. I gradually became more open to the acceptability of letting one's passion for God and for his purposes be clearly seen. I admit that, for myself, I remained more comfortable with 'in quietness and trust is your strength',[95] but then I'm British! As Marion always says, praying quietly in a loud prayer meeting is easier than praying loudly in a quiet one.

We did have some loud prayer meetings (my co-leader was gifted with a personality that was far less reserved than mine) but we were keen not to 'heap up empty phrases' thinking we'd 'be heard for [our] many words'.[96] In leading the prayer meetings we made sure our prayers were well targeted. We always sought out a Bible passage to define the direction of our praying. Tackling issues in prayer was new to many of us and we found the thought of bringing areas under God's control helpful. We found the book of Joshua especially useful. Its emphasis on taking territory was close to what we had in mind, especially when we underpinned it with the confidence of Psalm 24:1, 'The earth is the Lord's, and everything in it, the world, and all who live in it.' Ultimately, I'd say we saw ourselves as city

---

95. Isaiah 30:15.
96. Matthew 6:7 ESV.

builders rather than city takers, although at the time there was a new wave of songs coming out of churches in the States and Australia that emphasised spiritual warfare with a city-taking focus.

If there was a sense in which we were pioneering, we knew we weren't pioneering alone, but we saw the need to be responsible for the problems that were specific to London at the time. We picked three in particular: one relating to inequality, a second relating to abuse, and a third relating to civil unrest. I won't go into too much detail as everyone who sees a need for this kind of prayer strategy will have to identify their own root challenges. I'll just describe two of our breakthroughs by way of encouragement.

There was an association embedded within wider society that was having a lot of sway through its interconnectivity with the nation's major institutions, such as government, the media, the church and the courts. Its aim seemed to be to change society by maintaining a preference for an elite group held together by secrecy. For us, this was at odds with God's way of doing things transparently and seemed similar to the way people in Ephesus were bound together in their worship of Diana. We knew that in Ephesus Paul's strategy of teaching God's word eventually led to open confrontation.[97] We were trusting that having the confrontation take place through prayer would open everything up, removing the secrecy and allowing the light of God's good news to shine in. We weren't arrogant in praying like this. In fact our Bible knowledge led us to a blind and weakened Samson being led by a young servant to stand among the pillars of a foreign temple. Despite the cost to himself he pushes the pillars down.[98] We were aiming to break the secrecy within a society that had created its rituals around a temple we could read about in the

---

97. Acts 19:23-41.
98. Judges 16:25-29.

9. Persisting: Pursuing with passion

Bible that had pillars reflecting establishment and strength.[99] It seemed that God agreed with our focus, as week by week while we prayed we witnessed demands for openness coming from the very quarters where the secret influence of the society had been greatest.

A second area had to do with civil unrest due to arms and extremism. We were praying ahead of the Good Friday agreement in Northern Ireland and there was unrest in London. We not only prayed for arms caches to be found before they could be used for harm, but sought to address the wider issues of extremism in a society where thoughtfulness was increasingly being replaced by what at the time might have been labelled as media-hype. We were grateful that arms caches were discovered.

Whether or not the things we wrestled with were 'beasts', I'll leave you to judge. People vary on how they differentiate and interpret 'authorities', 'powers of this dark world' and 'spiritual forces of evil in the heavenly realms' that Paul subsequently wrote to the Ephesians about.[100] The issues we dealt with seemed to me to be rooted in earthly realities, but maybe they had back-up from 'forces of evil in the heavenly realms'. If that is so, let me say a few words about how grateful I am for a sentence Paul wrote to the Colossians when he was under house arrest in Rome. He tells us that God 'having disarmed the powers and authorities... made a public spectacle of them, triumphing over them by the cross'.[101]

The Diana/Artemis cult cemented together a huge amount of religious overlay from both Greek and Roman polytheistic cultures. The Hebrew Scriptures declare, 'Who among the gods is like you, Lord... majestic in holiness, awesome in glory, working wonders?'[102]

---

99. 1 Kings 7:15-21.
100. Ephesians 6:12.
101. Colossians 2:15.
102. Exodus 15:11.

This sets God in his rightful place. I get concerned when people behave as if God is almighty and as if other forces in the heavenly realms, that might consider themselves to be 'gods', are almost almighty. Fear can so easily take over from such miscalculations. I don't believe Paul was fearful in Ephesus. As well as writing to the Colossians from Rome, he also wrote to the Ephesians, and what he said to them then had been just as true while he was battling alongside them years before,

> [The] incomparably great power for us who believe . . . is the same as the mighty strength [God] exerted when he raised Christ from the dead and seated him at his right hand in the heavenly realms, far above all rule and authority, power and dominion, and every name that is invoked, not only in the present age but also in the one to come.[103]

That 'far above' would have settled things for Paul and it should settle things once and for all for us too.

So if God is supreme, where does the pressure that Paul spoke about actually come from? Pressure comes from the need for persistence. When writing from Ephesus to the Corinthians Paul states, 'I will stay on at Ephesus until Pentecost, because a great door for effective work has opened to me, and there are many who oppose me.'[104] Both the opposition and the open door can bring pressure.

Battles are rarely won with a single assault, whether they are in the heavenly realm or far more down to earth. Disarmed powers and authorities will still want to fight, in the same way as a mortally wounded devil proves slow to lie down and die. We know that God

---

103. Ephesians 1:19-21.
104. 1 Corinthians 16:8-9.

9. Persisting: Pursuing with passion

has paid a price for humanity's redemption, and it is sad that not all buy into that freedom, but even those who do continue as a work in progress. One day it will all be put right, but we are living in the interim and that means the victories of the cross and the triumphs of the resurrection need to be constantly reinforced as the ultimate victory is kept in sight. It's this persistent overcoming that makes the pursuit so demanding.

I've already mentioned the inspiration we gained from reading the book of Joshua, but the story of Gideon and the Midianites in Judges, which I've referred to in an earlier chapter, also continued to inspire us. Four chapters ago we left Gideon with his three hundred on the hills surrounding the Midianite camp, blowing their trumpets, shouting their shout, breaking their jars and shining their lights. Amazingly they then have the presence of mind to stand firm alongside Gideon as thousands re-mobilise to chase the fleeing Midianites. Eventually, when they do move and gather around Gideon as he congratulates the Ephraimite warriors for capturing two of the Midianite leaders, they know their task isn't over. The Bible describes them as 'exhausted yet keeping up the pursuit'. They are pursuing Zebah and Zalmunna, the kings of Midian, determined not to let things rest until their mission is complete.[105] Paul later demonstrates that tenacity in Ephesus, and we endeavoured to embrace it too. We wanted our praying to make a lasting difference. Ever since we'd been graciously labelled as 'the south gate' we'd been taking our gatekeeping responsibilities seriously. I was still believing for the river of life to sweep through the city to bring in the new, water the good, and flush out the unhelpful, but getting ahead of the

---

105. Judges 7:22 – 8:5.

flow and prayerfully shifting some of the things that would have to go was absolutely worthwhile.

Paul's task in Ephesus is massive and continues to stretch out before him. I'm sure that reasoning in the School of Tyrannus energises him, but the demands on him are far greater than that as God entrusts him with an extraordinary healing and deliverance ministry. The record in Acts gives the impression that the miracles are so amazing that they leave the congregation wondering how to reach those who are too sick to attend the meetings. This concern prompts them to stir up the faith of such people by bringing them items that Paul has touched. God then graciously responds to that simple trust by healing them.[106]

Contrary to what some people might think, handling the extraordinary is never easy. If you are determined that people should understand it's God who's the healer and that all the praise must go to him, being put on a pedestal, which isn't healthy at the best of times, can become extremely tiring. Dealing with it rightly demands stepping down from the pedestal – deliberately and publicly, and, if need be, repeatedly. But no sooner has he handled that than along come the exorcists. They have devised a new formula that involves Paul's name. Fortunately Paul doesn't have to deal with them directly as the demon they are trying to cast out confronts them for him. But it all adds to the pressure. What happens next, though, is incredible. £4,500,000 worth of sorcery material goes up in smoke in the town square.[107] It's a huge amount of money to have been spent on things that they now consider to be dangerous and worthless. How on earth were people tricked into paying so much for such trivialities? But some traders are remarkably slick, and religious manipulators are

---

106. Acts 19:11-12.
107. Acts 19:13-20. Note: a drachma is about a day's wage.

9. Persisting: Pursuing with passion

always around. There is value, though, in all that smoke because it shows the extent of people's repentance, and going forward, with the sales regime broken, there is the possibility of £4,500,000 remaining in people's pockets and £4,500,000 less getting into the hands of traders. But that isn't the point. It has been a hard-won fight and Paul has pursued it to a place of breakthrough. Things have shifted and Paul is feeling confident about moving on. He's even considering visiting Rome.[108] But not everyone is happy.

Not everyone may have been happy with us either, but internally things were going well and the only adjustments required were minor. We'll pause to reflect and then move on.

Question:

How important do you think it is to tackle in prayer some of the bigger issues that may be having an influence within your area of operation? How would you plan to do this and what would be your message in seeking to mobilise others?

---

108. Acts 19:21.

10. Coordinating: *Staying on track*

We had started broadcasting our services on television, and new recruits to our camera team needed training. We agreed to set aside a Saturday and make it an opportunity for would-be preachers as well as would-be camera operators. We planned to have our own form of a double-blind trial. The preachers could preach and the camera operators could film with neither of them knowing that I'd later be viewing all the footage. Once I'd looked through a few short sermons, I came to one recorded by a young man I'd had my eye on for future leadership. He began by describing a Monty Python sketch – a race for people with no sense of direction.[109] For him, it seemed to sum up our church.

Watching the sketch now on YouTube I have to smile. The track is plain for all to see, and so are the lane markings. The line-up is great and everyone has clearly been trained for a clean start. It looks good with all on their marks, but at the sound of the starting pistol, chaos is let loose. The participants run everywhere. I got the point our young preacher was trying to make, but unlike him I was not dismayed. In the church we had people who a few months earlier would never have had the motivation to run, let alone join a race, and it was amazing that they'd so quickly reached a point where they could achieve both. They even knew how to prepare themselves on the starting line, which I saw as another plus. Clarifying direction

---

109. Available on YouTube https://www.youtube.com/watch?v=qgSzGIkFq2A&ab (accessed 4.12.24).

would have been the next move. But maybe if I'd said that it could have been taken as a flippant response.

The race we as a church were encouraging people to run was open to all and the picture of people running here, there and everywhere spoke very differently to me from the way that it had spoken to our young preacher. I knew that most of our weekly sermons were designed to set people running, and although no-one in the sketch could be seen running straight ahead, I'm sure that just about everyone with us had a clear enough sense of direction to head straight for the tape. But one of our roles as a teaching centre was to help everyone rethink the way they were following Jesus. Were those who were powering their way down the track totally unaware of what was happening on the starting line? For me, being there for one another *is* 'church'. I think of church as a race in which we have to be willing at times to have others set the pace for us, just as at other times we'll be setting the pace for them. By nature I can be a little obsessive. I like tidiness, but I am not so obsessed as to ask everyone to stay in their own lane and run at the same speed. That might look tidy but I'd definitely prefer something more messy where beginners, strugglers and would-be ministry entrepreneurs are supported and encouraged by fellow runners. What we wanted was to see everyone running with each other in mind. Had those powering down the track failed to pick up the message? Were they oblivious to the beginners who were confused and heading off anywhere without having first established a clear sense of the ultimate goal? If so, we needed to redouble our efforts to establish peer partnerships.

But before turning to that, there was something else I was aware of from the YouTube video. We were also encouraging everyone to see that God can call us to specific assignments. So some of the

10. Coordinating: Staying on track

apparent haphazardness that our young would-be preacher had been concerned about may have been the result of people heading off to fulfil such callings while still on route for the finishing line. As I reached the end of his short sermon, I found myself thinking about coordination. How were we backing up our words from the platform with the way we were organising church? Were people aware of the need to support beginners, strugglers and 'ministry entrepreneurs'? Were they even aware of the concept of pacesetters or registered the benefits of running with each other in mind?

We don't know at what point Paul appointed elders and deacons at Ephesus but we know that he definitely made sure they were eventually in place.[110] His understanding was that elders had to be mature and trusted people who could make room for the ministry of others. In a similar way, deacons had to be both fit to serve and able to set an example.[111] From the day he arrived in Ephesus, I believe he'd have been looking for local people he could position with this in mind. When we relaunched, we had deacons who'd served well in previous situations, so we appointed them as elders, asking some to continue as trustees. At the same time we began looking for people to bring onto staff in ministry roles. In an energised church where individual initiative was prized, there was already a lot happening, including outreaches to different sectors of the community. We were seeking team members who could be encouragers. We wanted everyone to thrive in a positive environment, not only Sunday by Sunday but when they met with others in smaller groups or were out with everybody engaging in evangelism.

---

110. Acts 20:17. Some think that it was when Paul had moved on from Ephesus to Macedonia that he sent Timothy back to make these appointments. Others think that 1 Timothy applies to the responsibility of appointing additional elders and deacons after a later visit made by Paul beyond the narrative of the book of Acts.
111. 1 Timothy 3:1-12. *Unstoppable Church*, pp. 65-72.

We had some great group leaders, dynamic enough to meet the expectations of those looking for the same affirmation and inspiration we were seeking to bring on Sundays. We could tell, though, that some were finding it hard to affirm and inspire at the same time, preferring a supposedly more inspirational 'we're here to teach you' approach. We would have loved to have found ways around this but we were allocating new people to groups all the time, trying to come up with appropriate matches. Unfortunately, overload was a problem as we couldn't find and envision new group leaders quickly enough. This was partly because we were seeing an increase among those too young to have a place to hold a home meeting. We wanted our groups to be peer-sharing gatherings, and it would have been great if the young people we were drawing in were students living in halls of residence who could have supported each other. We were left hoping that the enthusiasm of Sundays would be sufficient to maintain the sense of affirmation, even if some of the groups treated our younger newcomers more dismissively than we would have preferred.

Appointing two assistant ministers was a big step forward for us. It introduced some coordination and added to the vision reinforcement that our elders were doing behind the scenes. We gave one assistant minister responsibility for evangelism and outward-facing ministries. The other was given responsibility for building relationships within the church. We felt that once they'd settled in we'd be in a good place. But the picture from our young preacher's sermon still slightly troubled me. We were generating more ministries than we could effectively oversee, and welcoming established ministries that wanted to come alongside us. There was absolutely no way we were going to have everyone running in the same lane but the thought of multiplying lanes was great. It would simply mean that we'd be advancing on a very wide front. Even so, it did mean that, given our concentration on a really strong central drive, some running in the outer lanes missed out on the support and profile they deserved. We wanted to show the world the best and the pressure to do that can have its downsides. Deciding to promote only that which is reckoned to be highly polished can lead to a lack of authenticity. It may also lead to some omissions, and we actually came close to missing out on one of the strongest features of Paul's ministry at Ephesus.

We were following Paul's commitment to establishing a teaching centre and raising up a church to resource the region, but were in danger of overlooking the fact that he was personally committed to providing support unstintingly for every individual, no matter how significant or insignificant they might have seemed to be in the eyes of others. Our justification, as much as we'd really thought it through, was that we hoped that everyone's problems would be solved through our weekly expository Bible teaching, keeping any pastoral work required behind the scenes to an absolute minimum. In reality this was ironic as we had access to excellent counselling input and could easily have had very effective counselling provision running alongside our teaching programme. We were so set on seeing everyone becoming high-functioning and highly effective that we feared creating a counselling-dependent ethos that might take us in an opposite direction. In time we did rectify this but we could have done so more quickly if we'd taken a look at what Paul was doing behind the scenes when establishing his teaching-centre-cum-regional-resource-centre in Ephesus. The full extent of what he'd been doing came out some months after he'd moved on and returned to talk to the Ephesian elders.

Having revisited Macedonia and Greece, he returns to Asia and meets up with the Ephesian elders at Miletus. What he shares with them about the breadth of his input is mind-blowing.[112] It was all accomplished in the face of opposition and an already overloaded work schedule. As I list it out now, I'll not only include his actions but add in the things that show his mindset:

- He taught house-to-house as well as publicly.
- He saw his life as being worth nothing compared with his God-ordained life-goals.
- He was totally committed to finishing his God-given task of testifying to God's grace.
- He made sure he put no-one's eternal destiny at risk by failing to preach the gospel.
- He prioritised shepherding and watching over God's flock.
- He ensured that his presence kept wolf-like advantage-takers at bay.
- He watched out for 'truth-distorters' and 'disciple-seekers' arising from within.
- He equipped people by constantly warning them, even with tears, of the challenges they'd face once he'd moved on.
- He coveted nothing, but worked with his hands to meet his needs and those of his team.
- He gave practical support to the weak and lived his life believing 'it's more blessed to give than receive'.

---

112. Acts 20:16-35.

10. Coordinating: Staying on track

It's clear that Paul never set himself above those he served. He dealt daily with flesh and blood realities, even though he knew that in doing so he was fighting on multiple fronts, spiritual as well as physical. And in doing this he was not unique. The Twelve had done the same before him. It's all too tempting for leaders today to look at the moment when the Twelve set themselves apart for prayer and the study of God's word and to claim that for themselves, but prior to delegating, the Twelve had definitely not been detached.[113] They were hands-on with the teaching, the finance, the food distribution and everything else involved in running a congregation of 5,000. Even one person with needs can be demanding and the Twelve were not going to be hard-hearted. These days it's tempting to put multiple layers of leadership in place to preserve space for prayer and studying God's word, but the risk is that where there are multiple layers of leadership, coordination can suffer. It stands to reason that efficiency goes down when messages being passed upwards have to go through many messengers. It's better, no matter how many or few the messengers, that such messages are intercepted as soon as possible by concerned and accessible leaders.

Finally, when talking about coordination let's note that Paul was not into micro-management. He gave people space and was expecting the elders he was talking to in Miletus to do the same. The early church was not hierarchical. It was a company of people who provided each other with support and encouragement, and had leaders who considered it their responsibility to set an example.[114] This is definitely what Paul was doing and what the Twelve had done before him. They took on huge responsibilities, practical as well as spiritual, and set a great example of how to lead. As leaders, they

---

113. Acts 6:2-4.
114. 1 Peter 5:1-4.

would have known that coordinating without setting an example can run the risk of everyone still doing what is right in their own eyes, and they'd have known too that replacing coordination with control will only make matters worse. There's an orderliness in God's diversity but chaos comes when selfish ambition is left unchecked. The example set by these early leaders continued to inspire us as we delegated. We involved our assistant ministers in administration and premises management, but let them know that they weren't the only ones who needed to be setting a Paul-like example. The Twelve were still example-setters after they had delegated and we were determined to reflect that too.

Whatever the project you are creating, or the congregation you are shaping, people matter. They deserve exemplary care and competent coordination. That way they can develop their gifts.

Question:

How would you draw the line between coordination and control, and how flat (i.e. non-hierarchical) a management structure would you be comfortable with?

Refining

Branding — Buffeting — Re-envisioning — Maturing

11. Branding: *Living with labels*

There's a saying, 'If it quacks like a duck, floats like a duck and waddles like a duck, it probably is a duck.'[115] That may be true, but not all birds are so readily identified. My wife Marion loves identifying birds, but when we walk together I often fail to stand still long enough to let her complete the identification process. I move on, the bird flies away and the mystery remains. I wish that moving forward had the same effect when people start labelling churches and church movements, but any snapshot identification just somehow seems to stick. The process, if it can be called such, is as lacking in nuance as labelling the duck. Sadly, I think we're now so used to it that we've learnt to live with it, but the trouble is that once a church or movement is labelled, any variation from the stereotype goes unnoticed and people see what they want to see. It seems that you're either being defined to be dismissed or defined to be copied in a way that will miss out key elements of who you are and what you're doing. Sometimes you're defined to be pilloried, which all too often was the experience for Paul. Given the original meaning of 'branding', it could be said, hopefully without being too cynical, that you can't be branded without getting burned.

We were defining ourselves as a teaching centre that was seeking to be a resource church, working with others to serve London. But that was a cumbersome definition and didn't line up with the definitions that were currently in vogue. The churches that

---

115. Variously attributed.

understood us best were Kensington Temple and KICC as they had similar aims and we were continuing to work with them around Mission to London. A pattern was developing with Bible colleges, guest speakers, conferences, ministers' events and media exposure. Kensington Temple had been around for many years, but thanks to its graciousness there was a lot of mutual respect. Paul, when planting the church in Ephesus, was not blessed with such local understanding. Those who understood him best were in Macedonia, Greece and Galatia, and even further afield in Syria, Cilicia and Judea. He kept contact with them as time allowed through letters and exchanges of personnel.

The labelling Paul experienced was quite personalised. Things had been tough when he started out in Cilicia. We don't know how the Gentiles branded him there, but many of his fellow Jews were so unsympathetic they had him flogged.[116] When he'd been with Barnabas in Galatia on his first missionary journey the two of them were hailed as 'gods', but shortly afterwards the same crowd was stoning Paul for heresy.[117] On his second missionary journey, when he was with Silas and Timothy in Macedonia, owners of a slave girl accused them of being Jews who were 'throwing our city into an uproar by advocating customs unlawful for us Romans to accept or practise'.[118] Moving on to a nearby city, the accusations became global, 'These men who have caused trouble all over the world have now come here.'[119] And it continued. In Athens he was labelled as a 'babbler', said to be 'advocating foreign gods'.[120] In Corinth the

---

116. 2 Corinthians 11:24-25.
117. Acts 14:11-19.
118. Acts 16:19-21.
119. Acts 17:6.
120. Acts 17:18.

11. Branding: Living with labels

charge was that of 'persuading the people to worship God in ways contrary to the law'.[121]

It seemed that everywhere Paul went he was labelled as a troublemaker, someone who was drawing people away from their established ways of worship and undermining their legalistic foundations, regardless of whether they were looking to Rome or to Moses. None of this should surprise us. People don't like to be disturbed or made to feel uncomfortable. There's a mindset that thinks that anything that challenges needs to be removed, and that the one who does the challenging needs to be eliminated too.

Things in Ephesus eventually come to a head for Paul when traders in the city find their income affected by a widespread rejection of idol worship. In labelling Paul, the spokesperson for the traders has quite a lot to say:

> You see and hear how this fellow Paul has convinced and led astray large numbers of people here in Ephesus and in practically the whole province of Asia. He says that gods made by human hands are no gods at all. There is danger not only that our trade will lose its good name, but also that the temple of the great goddess Artemis will be discredited; and the goddess herself, who is worshipped throughout the province of Asia and the world, will be robbed of her divine majesty.[122]

In the midst of the riot that follows, the city clerk speaks up for Paul and his team saying, 'You have brought these men here, though they have neither robbed temples nor blasphemed our goddess.'[123]

---

121. Acts 18:13.
122. Acts 19:26-27.
123. Acts 19:37.

I find the second part of his statement interesting as it throws light on how Paul preached the gospel. 'He reasoned with them from the Scriptures, explaining and proving that the Messiah had to suffer and rise from the dead.' He asserted that 'this Jesus I am proclaiming to you is the Messiah'.[124] I don't see Paul as someone who would deliberately seek to stir up a crowd by using endless negativity. It's generally better to preach 'for' than to constantly preach 'against', but either way can get us into trouble.

One of the things that led to labels for us was that Mission to London had a large advertising campaign and some fundraising strategies that many in the Church world considered tactless. We found the advertising bold and the fundraising equally so, but more importantly we were identifying with our brothers and sisters in their desire to present the gospel in the way they believed to be most effective. Being committed to help in any way we could, we could see labels coming our way. It's true that the conservative evangelical constituency with which I was linked was more questioning than the Pentecostal world around Kensington Temple or the African diaspora around KICC. This kind of branding, though, is not what I want to talk about. I'm more concerned about the kind of labelling that wants to brand you so as to copy you or claim you as its own.

One of the reasons why the copying and claiming kind of branding gets little attention is that for some pioneering people, being copied is the outcome they're hoping for. They're not too fussed about whether or not the copiers have understood the template correctly, and in some ways that's good. What we raise up is not ours to own. God has to be the starter and finisher of every project, and he

---

124. Acts 17:2-3.

11. Branding: Living with labels

can use what is his in any way he pleases.[125] If the offspring looks different from the parent, so be it.

Where I do become concerned is when branding starts to place an expectation on something original to make it conform to a stereotype in ways that ride roughshod over God's specific calling. There are many examples in the business world where a firm has become a franchise and its values have become compromised as the franchise overwhelms it. I'm not at all convinced that God wants every original project to be franchised or to be consumed by an existing one. At the beginning of this book I explained that there are projects and movements that will succeed precisely because those taking them forward have bought into something distinctive that's on God's agenda. Generally when God raises up a movement he doesn't have just one template on which to base it. It's the limitations of our human imagination that have us create a category and then cram everything into it.

This might be a good moment to make us think about the flipside of the duck identification analogy. Let's think of a bird, any bird. Now let's say to that bird, 'We're calling you a duck so you must quack like a duck, float like a duck and waddle like a duck.' It would be a crazy thing to do, but hopefully the very suggestion leaves us in no doubt as to what I'm talking about. But just to push the point a little further, if we as church leaders and active church members were to take up birdwatching, would we, with our love of categorisation, end up creating quacking blackbirds, floating sparrows and waddling skylarks? All too often our thinking is, 'Now we've labelled you, you have to fit!'

---

125. Hebrews 12:2; Philippians 1:6.

I'm sure that what God has called you to do is special for him as well as for you, and if he'd wanted something done differently he would have made that clear and probably chosen someone else to do it. That's why I'm often reluctant to link emerging strategists with people who've done nearly the same thing before them, or (perhaps even worse) nearly done the same thing before them. Once I knew what God had called me to do, and I had the right people around me to do it, we just set out to achieve it together.

In doing this I was deliberately 'staffing to my weaknesses'. I had a co-leader who was considerably younger than I was and was blessed with different gifts. As new trends developed around us, I believed that as a team we were discerning enough to find appropriate levels of engagement. One growing category at the time was that of the megachurch. It was something of an umbrella term, but it was giving space for new churches with a big vision, a big team and the energy to raise finance for significant premises. Apostolic and prophetic were also terms that were being bandied around. Notionally, 'apostolic church' implied a strong visionary leader and 'prophetic church' indicated a leader prepared to challenge complacency. Many churches sought to combine the two, seeing the dual gifting in the leader and believing it would flow down through the congregation.

Perhaps the most confusing terms, though, were 'cutting edge' and 'breakthrough'. They acknowledged that God was doing something new but the risk for the churches taking up such labels was that once they'd arrived at what was deemed to be the 'cutting edge', or 'broken through' the barrier they believed to be most in need of obliterating, they could just end up frozen in the style of the moment. 'Megachurches', 'Apostolic Churches', 'Cutting-edge Churches', 'Apostolic and Prophetic Churches', 'Breakthrough Churches'

11. Branding: Living with labels

... We were invited to speak at them all, and in each case we were labelled as 'one of us'.

In our minds, however, we were very much a gateway church. Not just because we'd been labelled that by Kensington Temple, but because we'd embraced the role. We were serious about what came in and out of London and about the spiritual forces at work within it. Furthermore, we were providing a platform for speakers from overseas and this increasingly defined us as an entry point. We had a regular television programme and a wide network of contacts, and both seemed attractive to those wanting to gain exposure in the UK.

We welcomed speakers from East Africa, West Africa, the United States, the Caribbean, Asia and Australia. In line with global church interests at the time, some brought an apostolic and prophetic emphasis, while others, especially those leading megachurches or broadcasting on global television networks, tended to emphasise personal empowerment. We were grateful for what they taught, and as the majority of the teaching still rested with my co-leader and me, we felt we were able to maintain a balanced output, both in the leisure centre and on television. The fact that when teaching ourselves we favoured six-week-long series of Bible-based teaching on a comprehensive range of scriptural themes, helped enormously. We were determined that the south gate would be a Bible gate. It had to be if we were to fulfil an Acts 19 teaching-centre vision.

Not surprisingly, we made a point of socialising with our guest speakers so that they were able to understand our vision. We were prepared to be completely transparent and I guess that enabled those who wanted to use us as a platform to have a really good look at us. We were used to being pigeon-holed (or, to use my earlier illustration, duck-labelled), but wanted to make sure that we wouldn't be superficially branded by those who knew us well.

We wanted to be accepted for who we were and for what we were endeavouring to do. But maybe those seeking a platform (or perhaps even those planning a franchise) look for different things from those seeking a gateway. As it turned out, we were under closer scrutiny than we realised. But this would be a good point to pause and reflect.

Question:

How important do you think it is to be able to differentiate between those who might be defining you to dismiss you and those who may be defining you to copy you or own you?

12. Buffeting: *Cultural cross-currents*

I want to set the right tone for this chapter. The story is simple enough, but interpretations could vary. I'll start with an incident that really belongs in the timeframe of *Unstoppable Church*, the first book in this series. It tracks back to a time when I was working as a junior member of a maxillofacial surgical team in a London teaching hospital. We were in the operating theatre and the lead surgeon asked the theatre supervisor for a particular surgical instrument. It was handed over in the usual slap-into-glove way and greeted by the surgeon with a look that could be read quite clearly despite the mask. His eyes said it all, utter incredulity! 'What has happened to this?' he asked as calmly as he could. 'I've had it straightened,' the theatre supervisor replied. 'But it was already the shape it was supposed to be,' was the response that went through our minds as we hid our gaze in embarrassed silence. I guess it's the 'it was already the shape it was meant to be' that I want you to hold onto.

We, as a church, had just started committing a small amount of money each month to a particular American ministry. We wanted to encourage the servant-hearted people who were running its UK base. Somehow the word went around that everything we were doing as a church was now being placed into American hands. The timing of this couldn't have been worse. At the precise moment we started giving, some UK-based ministries well-known for their monitoring abilities, decided to launch a specific attack on this particular American ministry. We ended up with people leaving simply because ... well ... people were leaving! I heard some say we were becoming a 'fruitless tree', a slogan they'd picked up from articles circulating against the American ministry. It didn't occur to them that they were causing the appearance of fruitlessness by persuading people to leave.

Now it's interesting that before the riot in Ephesus, Paul has already decided to move on. Initially he has thought of going straight to Corinth but on reflection feels the church there needs time to work through the counsel he's given in his letter.[126] His new plan involves travelling north and once again crossing to Macedonia from Troas, sailing via Samothrace into Neapolis. He has even sent Timothy and Erastus to Macedonia ahead of him.[127] If the would-be rioters had known this, maybe they could have saved themselves some trouble. But that doesn't seem to be the way it works. If people are nursing a complaint, they will bring it, regardless of who's around to hear it.

My co-leader and I were away on a two-week overseas mission trip when the departures began in earnest. As he stayed on to be joined by his wife for a holiday, I returned alone. I was aware that Paul's team had kept him out of the amphitheatre during the riot,[128] and that made me think there must be more than one way of handling a problem. I wasn't sure what to do but I felt terribly concerned and began thinking things through on my own, weighing the wisdom or otherwise of us both being away at the same time, and blaming myself for what I saw as a pastoral failure. By the time my co-leader returned, I'd convinced myself that I should take more responsibility at home and that he should fulfil our travelling responsibilities on his own. I can still remember how I came to this conclusion and

---

126. 2 Corinthians 1:15 – 2:4.
127. Acts 19:21-22.
128. Acts 19:30.

12. Buffeting: Cultural cross-currents

regret now that I'd arrived at it with none of the joint thinking we'd become known for. My proposal involved sacrifice for both of us; probably more for him than for me as it moved the leadership responsibility more in my direction, but he graciously accepted it. It was not great to find myself alone, exercising a pastoral and teaching ministry without the excitement of the joint leadership I'd been used to. Nonetheless, I believed we were still very much a team even though at times I knew we would be in different parts of the world.

The situation at home was getting complicated. More theological questions were publicly circulating around a growing number of American ministries. I've mentioned Paul's skill in writing to the Corinthians, saying it reminded me of Elisha's handful of flour.[129] Well, as the cry of 'death in the pot' grew louder, disturbing more and more well-meaning UK churches, I was determined not to kick over the pot but to find the handful of flour. Elisha knew that the traumatised sons of the prophets needed careful handling. I had to think of those in the Ministers' Fellowship, as well as those in our local congregation. I decided to tread carefully and to maximise our role as a teaching centre, using an approach that could be summed up as 'some say this, and some say that, but the best way to see it from Scripture is this'. Week after week, the teaching stayed really simple, working through key issues while strengthening people's relationship with God through Jesus. Admittedly the calming effect would have been greater if my co-leader and I had been preaching side-by-side but, as indicated, he was away fulfilling the wider requests that were coming in for both of us. Finding the handful of flour seemed to be down to me. But then, out of the blue, my

---

129. 2 Kings 4:38-41.

co-leader and I had the opportunity to come together to speak at a conference overseas.

The prospect of working together again really appealed, but I wondered if it was too soon for me to start travelling again. I tried to present our would-be host with one or two conditions around my side of the programme, pointing out that it was always my wish to include more remote areas and that I would like him to join me. This was initially agreed, but later left unfulfilled. I sensed it was going to be a tricky trip. It was even more strange on arrival as our host was clearly convinced he was about to do something that would prove to be a big favour, not only to the two of us but also to our church. He'd apparently consulted quite widely behind the scenes to formulate his plan. When my co-leader and I had some downtime together in our hotel, we had to admit that we were facing some bizarre allocations as to which of us should speak when at his conference. One night we were kept up really late in our host's office, listening to him advising us to go further with our separation of roles. He wanted us to formalise my co-leader's responsibility for our travelling engagements, putting them into a separate ministry. It seemed that he and others had concluded that, by failing to meet age-related honour expectations within our shared leadership, we'd been exhibiting cultural confusion and creating a double-headed monster that we both needed to be rescued from.

As I had requested, I did preach more remotely, but on my own, and afterwards had lunch with a church leader based in the city from where I'd be heading for international departures and home. As I shared with him something of what I expected to be working through on my return, he told me that I'd only heard half the plan. He laughed at my ignorance and explained the rest of what he

12. Buffeting: Cultural cross-currents

understood lay in store for me. I flew out of the country convinced that he'd got it wrong. It was just too crazy to be true.

Paul didn't have Silas with him in Ephesus, but they'd worked well together in Cilicia, Galatia, Macedonia and Greece. As far as I could see their leadership partnership had never been branded as a double-headed monster. Partnership was not a problem for me in the way it appeared to be for others. I had no problem with equality and was discovering that I didn't really appreciate the dividing of roles we'd recently had to agree to. Why couldn't we continue assuming we were equally experienced and equally enthusiastic, even if in reality we were still working towards it from different positions of strength? Despite these thoughts, we decided to go ahead with the suggestion to formalise a separate travelling ministry, and gathered our friends around us for an official launch. It was a privilege to have senior leaders from West Africa, East Africa and the United States join us, but in some of the congratulatory messages there were echoes of what I'd been told at the end of my recent trip – this was not to be just a new ministry but a new church, eventually with half of our members meeting in a venue likely to be just a few miles down the road. Even at the ministry launch I still didn't believe it. I just assumed my co-leader was as much in the dark about the idea as I was, but as the days went by, regardless of whether he knew about the plan or not, I became more and more sympathetic to the thought of him having space to work things through on his own. Our partnership had very much tied him into me and my vision, and he was more than capable of leading without me, but I knew I would miss him and that the church would never be the same without his gifts alongside mine.

In all of this there was an irony. I sensed that anyone thinking that the church would be a more suitable platform for their ministry without our co-leadership was going to be disappointed. If they were looking for connectivity and experience, I could provide that, but there was a flare that my co-leader possessed that just wasn't my style. I'd also be inclined to let pastoral concerns overload me to the detriment of impact, proclamation and presentation. I'd be longing for excellence whilst being too pastoral to insist on it, preferring simply to set an example of high standards in the hope of inspiring an appropriate uptake. We both loved to teach and I was happy to teach in front of a crowd, but I never saw myself as a crowd-creator. Together we were an interesting pairing, a combination of energy, enthusiasm and experience. If the church were to divide, depending on who went with whom, we could end up with two very different churches.

In the end we did lose about half the church, plus the assistant ministers and eventually two of the elders. This was probably to be expected as we'd been functioning as a joint leadership. But did that mean the grace God had given us to fulfil the task had also been halved, or, as some people verbalised it, had the anointing left with my co-leader? I had to come to terms with this. I sensed I'd lost a ministry partner rather than a ministry anointing. If there was an anointing for leading a vibrant, youthful megachurch, I wanted to release it and find contentment in being left with whatever God should choose to bless me with.

Actually, it didn't work out like that. As the Bible says, 'God's gifts and his call are irrevocable.'[130] The callings on our lives remained, as did God's giftings. Even so, there was so much I had to let go of, and there were times when I feared that I could be clinging to things in a wrong way. The story that Nathan told to King David

---

130. Romans 11:29.

12. Buffeting: Cultural cross-currents

about the rich man who'd taken a poor neighbour's lamb so he could feed a traveller kept coming to mind.[131] It took me ages to work out whether I was the poor man who'd lost the lamb or the rich man who'd stolen it. Most of the time I thought I must have been the rich man, because, although I'd lost much, I still appeared to have so much more than my co-leader who was starting afresh with next to nothing. The thought of holding onto something I needed to be releasing did cause me concern.

Paul had to trust so much into the hands of others, and I was having to do the same: people, partners, vision, reputation, contacts and hopes for the future, but the key was to do it with good grace, and to ignore those who were advising differently. My aim had to be to follow Paul's example in Acts 20:2 to move on (at least figuratively), travelling 'through [the] area, speaking many words of encouragement to the people'.

The buffeting was tough but God was good, and I've never reproached the ministry-reshapers who took things into their own hands. It did feel as if something that had been working well had been taken away and hammered flat by those who never understood the nuances of what we'd set up or were seeking to achieve, but maybe I played a part in that too. Yet who was I to say that God couldn't use what would emerge from the reshaping, and good things did emerge. So, please don't dismiss this chapter. It's not been an easy one for me to write and I hope I have written it fairly, reflecting how I understood things at the time. Others, of course, have the right to see the whole episode very differently. All in all, it may seem a strange chapter to include in what is basically a help manual for people thinking of setting up a strategic church project

---

131. 2 Samuel 12:1-4.

or a strategic ministry project, but we all need to know that setbacks can occur. The good news is that we can now go on to talk about how to survive them. But please, if you're tempted to reshape someone else's ministry, remember that God is the One who is well able to perfect what he has begun.[132]

The final two chapters of this book are about re-envisioning and maturing, and as they are the two principal ways of surviving a setback they rightly deserve a chapter each.

Question:

What would you have done in this, or a similar, situation? What can you learn from how I handled it?

---

132. Philippians 1:6; Hebrews 12:2.

13. Re-envisioning: *Recasting the net*

A riot just as Paul is about to leave is inconvenient to say the least. It is not the exit he has been planning. There have been plenty of times when he has left a city as public discord erupts, but that has never been his ideal. His preference is always to leave the believers in good shape with a measure of respect from the local authorities. He recalls achieving this in Philippi. When the magistrates wanted him to leave prison quietly and make his way out of the city, he had them come to escort him out, allowing him to say farewell to his friends before moving on.[133] He also left Corinth calmly after a significant stay, and thought he'd be doing the same after a few years in Ephesus. Actually, as it happens, he will be leaving the church in Ephesus in a better state than he may have realised. He has long been confident that they could cope without him in the midst of calm but now, as the riot is reaching its climax, he discovers that they can cope without him in the midst of chaos. Much as he wants to go into the arena to resolve the matter, he is restrained so as to leave it to others.[134] There comes a moment when we have to accept that we are not indispensable, and setbacks are a particularly good time to take this on board. In the end Demetrius the silversmith and riot-raiser is not Paul's problem.[135] Going forward, it is the church that has to shoulder the load for a new season.

It was going to be a new season for us too, and that meant it was time to recast the vision. As I was preparing to do this I thought

---

133. Acts 16:35-40.
134. Acts 19:30.
135. Acts 19:23-27.

of the risen Jesus standing on the shore of Galilee, calling out to a dispirited boatful of fishermen who'd fished all night and caught nothing. What was in their minds as a voice rang out across the water? 'Throw your net on the right side of the boat and you'll find some.'[136] It sounded simple enough, but the men in the boat were dog-tired and the net was wet and heavy. It would take some effort to haul it in, and then summon up their combined strength to fling it out so that it opened to its fullest extent. Nonetheless, they did it, even though they had yet to recognise the caller.

I really admired their recasting effort and was preparing myself for the same task. In some ways nothing had changed. It was the same net, the same ship and we were fishing in the same sea. Maybe the pace had changed, but the vision hadn't. We still wanted to change London through teaching God's word. The college, the guest speakers, the systematic teaching on Sundays, the teaching weeks, the television programmes, the overseas travel, the Ministers' Fellowship, the public proclamation, the friendship evangelism were all still relevant. We were very conscious of the first verse of Psalm 127 as we prayed into the future:

> Unless the LORD builds the house,
>   the builders labour in vain.
> Unless the LORD watches over the city,
>   the guards stand watch in vain.

But the second verse was gaining relevance too:

---

136. John 21:6.

13. Re-envisioning: Recasting the net

> In vain you rise early
>   and stay up late,
> toiling for food to eat –
>   for he grants sleep to those he loves.

I was feeling God's hand on my life and I was going to feel it even more firmly once the vision had been recast. I longed to retain the energy, enthusiasm and excellence that we'd sought to make our hallmark. I wanted to say to everyone, as I'd said earlier to the Ugandans, 'Who's willing to go faster?', but I felt constrained. Maybe we were going to find a different expression of energy, enthusiasm and excellence.

Casting vision is exactly like casting a net. As you throw it out, it has to go wide, and you need to see every inch of it opening up before you. Recasting is even more complicated than simply casting. The net has already become saturated, and if that can be overlooked while it's over the side, as soon as it's hauled into the boat its weight is felt by all. We'd originally cast our vision with a great flourish, and had made sure that everything we had in mind for the future could be seen, at least in potential. My aim now was to convince everyone that the gains we'd made were not only going to be sustained but used to greater advantage.

I knew I had to make the church feel secure. This, though, was particularly hard for me since, as I implied earlier, I would have preferred to have made it feel exciting; but most of those who would have stood alongside me to prioritise excitement over security were now standing alongside my former co-leader a few miles down the road. I consoled myself with the fact that there was at least one exciting church in the area. Meanwhile, I faced up to the needs of those who were still around me. My default position became 'maximum participation with minimum pressure'. As I worked to make this happen, it began to feel as if, after four-and-a-half years of hectic activity, this was actually the right approach. It might even have been what we would have been doing if we'd still been working with the same delivery team and the same congregation.

In changing pace, I realised we might be risking the loss of the cutting-edge/breakthrough label that some had pinned on us. Then I thought that perhaps 'sustainable church' might be the new cutting-edge and that achieving stability might be seen as the latest breakthrough. If 'stable' and 'sustainable' were on God's heart, then maybe we were becoming even more truly apostolic and prophetic than we'd ever been. But as I've already said, labels have never really been my thing as I can see their capacity for imposing limitations.

While we were recasting our vision, the new church down the road was pressing on with its journey of launching, expanding, partnering, engaging, persisting and coordinating. Being in the congregation as they dedicated their impressive new premises felt both special and strange. As my former co-leader was revealing to all his undoubted effectiveness as a church planter and church leader, I could reflect on the would-be church planters who were beginning to head in our direction from around London. They saw us as a safe place to work through their positioning, waiting and assessing as they prepared themselves for their moment of vision-sharing. To be honest I hadn't seen this coming, although I should have done. It was a major part of the Ephesus vision that I'd missed.

No one knows exactly how and when the other six churches of the Roman province of Asia, as addressed in the book Revelation, came into being. Maybe people visited the School of Tyrannus from Smyrna, Pergamum, Thyatira, Sardis, Philadelphia and Laodicea. Perhaps some even came from Colossae in nearby Phrygia. But

13. Re-envisioning: Recasting the net

there is no doubt that in the end, Asia was not just hearing God's word from the church in Ephesus but from the churches in Smyrna, Pergamum, Thyatira, Sardis, Philadelphia and Laodicea too.[137] It was not so much that the river of life that flowed through and from the church in Ephesus had divided into branches. Each church had its own life source, releasing a stream of transformation into the region.

I knew from the outset that I was not looking at raising branch churches. Seeing churches come into being that could stand in their own right, with their own strong spiritual source of supply was an altogether different proposition. In our first four-and-a-half years there were one or two church leaders who'd repeatedly visited our Sunday services, thinking they might be more relevant for them in their stage of development than our Ministers' Fellowship. By contrast, in this new phase, would-be leaders were not just visiting but coming to journey with us for a season, wanting to be mobilised along with everyone else. We didn't need to hold special church planting programmes, we were mobilising the whole church in a way designed to turn followers of Jesus into leaders for Jesus.[138]

It's quite something when you are seeking to recast a vision for others and end up having God recast the vision for you. If that personal shift hadn't happened, I would probably have struggled with some of the changes we had to fit into our new phase of church life. There seemed to be a whole series of circumstances coming against us. Within a relatively short space of time we had to move on from the leisure centre (except for baptisms). We had to relocate the Bible college and to rethink our small-group programme. It was hard, but God was clearly in control. As each issue was resolved, it enabled us to bring a stronger aspect of training into our church life.

---
137. Revelation 1:4; 2:1 – 3:22.
138. See *Unstoppable Church*, pp. 39-45.

And by training I'm not meaning specialist training for a few, but effective discipleship training for all. Having embraced the concept of maximum mobilisation with minimum pressure, and having always believed that God was in the business of turning followers of Jesus into leaders for Jesus, putting teaching and training together was beginning to make perfect sense.

So how did it work out in practice? Well, I really didn't want to let go of the performance suite in the leisure centre. I loved the fact that it was open to the public and that the tiered seating kept everyone in view. The tiered seating also stopped church feeling like being on a bus waiting for the conductor to collect the fares. I know I haven't been saying much about finance in this book, but that's because I believe that getting the ministry right has to be the priority. Too many seek first the finance rather than seeking first the kingdom; we had undoubtedly picked up some unhelpful offering-appeal habits along the way. I do think that offerings have an important place in our worship, but targeted appeals also have their place, both in our personal worship and in our corporate fundraising. They work better away from the public arena and for these we tended to hold vision nights.

Although being appropriate with offerings in a public meeting is something that has always concerned me, having greater freedom to encourage giving was definitely not the reason we left the leisure centre. We left the leisure centre because a new company took over the franchise and claimed they didn't have time to reset the performance suite between Saturday nights, which required an empty floor and disco lights, and Sunday afternoon, which needed tiered seating and stage lighting. With broadcasting commitments to fulfil we had no option other than to move.

13. Re-envisioning: Recasting the net

It was good that we had a long lease at a reasonable rate on our town-centre basement. It proved possible to reconfigure the sports hall we'd created into an auditorium with a low stage and seating on three sides, some of it raised. Amazingly, it not only offered a far more convenient layout for filming services, but as it was 'our space' it gave everyone coming to church a greater opportunity to feel they belonged. This is something I probably would have missed if God hadn't recast my thinking towards a more intimate style of church. In the change we not only took the opportunity of encouraging key people in our television department to go on and establish their own channels, but also to relocate the Bible college. We found it easier to deliver the course on a one-evening-a-week basis by moving it from central London to our repurposed centre.

Perhaps the biggest contribution to creating a training emphasis was rethinking our programme for small groups. There are a number of Bible verses where a misreading can make a priority of personal gain. One of these is, 'Seek first his kingdom and his righteousness, and all these things will be given to you as well.'[139] We decided to concentrate on the first part of the verse and call the replacement for our small group programme 'Kingdom First'. Its emphasis was to be on growing through contributing. We'd always had a problem with training enough leaders to cope with our constant flow of newcomers and the number of newcomers didn't go down when we left the public venue. However, some who'd been leading groups for us were no longer with us and it was clear that, among those leaders who remained, some preferred pastoral work and others preferred running meetings. We decided to split the roles and put separate coordinators in place for training and pastoring. This immediately

---

139. Matthew 6:33.

increased our mobilisation and reduced pressure as more people shared the load. We then further reduced pressure on people's homes by bringing people into the centre on different nights of the week and offering hospitality centrally. The aim throughout was to make sure that every receiver became a contributor.

Those we appointed as Kingdom First leaders were really meeting-facilitators. They had the responsibility week-by-week of appointing a different hospitality person, a different worship leader, a different feedback person and a different talk presenter, as well as finding several different prayer group leaders per session. The programme, excluding refreshments, would run for about eighty minutes, starting with forty minutes of prayer in groups using a topics list based on a Scripture passage, and then move into ten to fifteen minutes of sung worship (not led by one of the church worship team but by any church member, drawing on musical help as required), and then the feedback person would give a five-minute summary of the message they had heard on the Sunday, before someone would give a twenty-minute talk they'd prepared on a given topic. The Kingdom First leader would enthusiastically encourage the contributors through this process each week. It quickly became the norm for everyone to be encouraging everyone else. People clapped each other loudly knowing that their turn would come. Needless to say I just contributed to the applause and prayed along with everyone else in one of the prayer groups. I loved people's nonprofessional worship leading and heard some great messages, but more often than not the highlight for me was hearing the feedback from Sunday's sermon. Sometimes, if it were my message that was being reported on, I'd wonder if we'd been in the same service (which really made me think hard about my communication skills). At other times I heard my sermon preached better in five minutes than I'd managed in

13. Re-envisioning: Recasting the net

considerably longer (again, a check on my communicating ability – one I'd recommend all preachers to try).

The pastoral system now ran parallel to our new highly contributive midweek meetings. It was quite simple. When someone new visited the church and filled in a welcome card we allocated them to the contact person covering their postcode. We made sure we had contact people spread throughout south-east London and all of them were equipped to reach out and befriend those allocated, informing them of all that the church could offer. They would also say which evening people from their postcode area attended the Kingdom First programme. If they were alerted to pastoral needs, they could inform the pastoral coordinator, who could pass it on to the staff member with pastoral responsibility. Local contact people also had lists of the various teams that those joining the church could contribute to. There were high-quality display boards produced by our staff and media department to show how everything in the church was coordinated.

Our whole Kingdom First programme could be summed up in two words: 'caring' and 'declaring'. At the same time, though, the two words that had for a long time been summing our overseas missionary programme, 'sending' and 'supporting', were gaining new possibilities. We don't know how the would-be church planters were trained in Ephesus but those with such aspirations in our midst who'd engaged with the Kingdom First programme alongside everyone else were beginning to feel sufficiently well positioned and equipped to start sharing their vision with prospective members of their new congregations.

I feel that having given so much detail about a particular way of doing things that worked for us, I should move away from the details to draw out the principles. I think there are three. If you suffer a setback, allow yourself time to recover and get well beyond any resentment that could contaminate others. Secondly, in preparing to recast your vision, be open to the possibility of God recasting aspects of the vision to you. Thirdly, be very mindful of the people who are with you. They matter to your project and your ministry. Make sure you meet their needs, trusting that those who may have moved on will have their needs met elsewhere.

Question:

If you ever have to recast your vision, what would be your guiding principles?

14. Maturing: *A necessary step forward*

I was in my late teens heading to a university Christian Union weekend. I'd missed most of it but was determined to be there for the Sunday. I caught an early train from the station near my parents' home in Sussex to the station near the conference centre in Kent. Unfortunately, the stations were joined by what must have been the slowest section of rural track in the network. There were times when even the cows in the adjacent fields were overtaking us. Maybe the track has now closed and become a footpath, which may have speeded things up a bit. I knew the speakers for the weekend were going to be looking at John's first letter, so I decided to read it through on the train. I read it quite quickly but quick was still not a word I could apply to the train. There was no one in the carriage to talk to so I looked out of the window for a while and then read John's first letter again. It was a pattern I repeated until the train eventually crawled into my destination station.

It was a long and brisk walk to the conference centre and I arrived in time to hear the morning speaker talk about 1 John 2:2, but it was 1 John 2:12-14 that was troubling me after the journey. Why was John repeating himself across these three verses, addressing children, fathers and young men and then going over the same ground again? I just didn't get it. And what kind of progression is it age-wise that moves from being strong, having the word of God in you and overcoming the evil one, to simply knowing 'him who is from the beginning'? Years later I was still asking the same question, resolutely holding off anyone who approached me saying, 'I see you as my spiritual father.' It was a concept I felt so uneasy about that it all but made me determined not to grow up. My problem was that I couldn't see the difference between having the ability to be a spiritual father and insisting on being regarded as one.

I think that when Jesus said to the crowds and his disciples, 'Do not call anyone on earth "father",'[140] he was giving sound advice (family relationships, of course, excepted). I think more church-based relationships have gone astray through someone senior making status an issue, than through status being graciously set aside. The New Testament model of leadership is to lead by example from the centre while inspiring others to journey alongside. All of this was familiar territory for me, but what I hadn't realised, until so much got stripped away from me soon after the recasting, was just how much God actually values maturity. I'm naturally a buoyant person and have tried to share that buoyancy throughout this book, but for a season when all manner of things were being unleashed upon us, all I felt I had left was my experience and a small measure of maturity. Even added together they felt very little. Somehow they proved to be enough, but only because God is good at blowing on flickering flames so they can begin to create some warmth and shed some light.

Let's take a closer look at this learning period by facing a difficult question. When problems come, how much should we blame the devil? My answer is 'as little as possible'. Even if he is to blame, it's better not to let him gloat over what he'll be seeing as success. James 4:7 says, 'Resist the devil, and he will flee from you.' It doesn't say, 'Resist the devil and he will fly at you.' After a number of negative things came our way at once, I was more inclined to point to the

---

140. Matthew 23:9.

14. Maturing: A necessary step forward

wisdom that James describes as 'earthly' and 'unspiritual' rather than focus on any source beyond that.[141] After all, James says that earthly wisdom can unleash disorder, and it was certainly disorder that came our way. Problems arose when our basement building was flooded because of a massive leak from the adjacent boiler room serving the block of flats that towered above us. The drying-out process took months and when the flooring was ripped up, fungal spores got into our building's ventilation system and eventually found their way into my lungs. Diagnosing the cause of my chest pain, coughing and debilitation proved difficult. With symptomatic treatment I recovered enough to lead a prayer conference in Plateau State, Nigeria, but was taken ill on the flight home and found my output reduced, albeit with lessening degrees of severity, for the next five years. Recovery began when I started a graduated exercise programme following a whiplash injury in a shunt accident eleven months after the Nigeria trip.[142] Throughout this time the church had four services a Sunday and I was managing to preach at the first two, invite in a guest for the third and leave the fourth to the congregation. Most weeks then involved a lot of rest, which was increasingly being interspersed with exercises prescribed for me by my physiotherapist. A slow weekly walk by some water became a priority. My fellow walker would pick me up in his car and drop me off later. I remember how we celebrated the first day I actually made it all the way around a lake.

So what did I actually learn? Well, I've already shared a little of what I gleaned from Psalm 127, and the fact that I found walking by water so helpful may already have prompted you to think of Psalm

---

141. James 3:14-17.
142. I realise that graduated exercise therapy is no longer endorsed as a treatment for chronic fatigue as it can worsen symptoms for some, but I'm grateful that it worked for me.

23. If so, you'd be right. My starting point, though, was actually Matthew 11:28 which records Jesus speaking of two types of rest. The first is the rest he gives when we come to him weary from struggling with life's burdens. The second is the rest we find when we take on his yoke and learn from him. For me, Psalm 23 doesn't read like the song of an adolescent shepherd boy but as the record of a life well lived in the context of this second rest. At this time I learnt three important lessons from Psalm 23. The first relates to the words 'he makes me lie down in green pastures'.[143] At times it was as if I could sense God holding me down to rest in a place where I was surrounded by the abundance of his provision. The second comes from 'he guides', which I contrasted with 'even though I walk'.[144] I could see there had been moments when I'd been more interested in my walking than in his guiding, and those had been the occasions when I'd been more likely to wander into trouble. Reassuringly there's still the promise that he'll stay alongside and we'll find his correction comforting. The third is linked to 'he prepares'. It's addressed to God as an acknowledgement: 'You prepare a table before me in the presence of my enemies.'[145] What an extraordinary thing for God to do, but how typical of him. It's not about waiting until we're sure our enemies are defeated; it's when we're in the midst of them that he'll shift our focus by spreading a banquet before us.

Paul tells us that he knew what it was to be comforted by God after all the pressures of Ephesus. When writing to the Corinthians from Macedonia he speaks of 'the Father of compassion and the God of all comfort, who comforts us in all our troubles'.[146] He doesn't say exactly how God did the comforting but I'm sure he, as

---

143. Psalm 23:2.
144. Psalm 23:3,4.
145. Psalm 23:5.
146. 2 Corinthians 1:3-4.

14. Maturing: A necessary step forward

always, found hope in the scriptures and appreciated the support of his team as he travelled. On arriving in Macedonia, the news he received from Titus, whom he'd sent to Corinth to follow up on his letter from Ephesus, clearly lifted his spirit. With Paul's experience in mind, I began to think that my battle with the chest infection and the prolonged period of physical weakness probably had more to do with God settling me in a place of calmness after the comings and goings that led to the re-envisioning rather than the consequences of a flooded boiler room. What I did know was that pressing on played just as much a part in my recovery process as it surely did in Paul's. Even so, there was one more attitude shift I had to undergo if I were to see the recast vision fulfilled in the way God wanted. It takes us back to 1 John 2:12-14 and we can get there by way of the remaining verses of Psalm 127:

> Children are a heritage from the LORD,
>   offspring a reward from him.
> Like arrows in the hands of a warrior
>   are children born in one's youth.
> Blessed is the man
>   whose quiver is full of them.
> They will not be put to shame
>   when they contend with their opponents in court.

These final verses are not random. They relate back to the house builders and city watchmen whom the early verses imply are wise enough to labour in partnership with the Lord and to benefit from the rest he brings. If we look back to Genesis 14:14 where Abram mobilises his household to rescue his nephew, Lot, there are those he describes as 'born in his household'. I like this expression as it widens the understanding of 'children'. Somehow it feels safer when church leaders think of church members as 'children of the house' rather than seeing everyone as products of their personal ministry. The same is true when project leaders speak in a similar way of those who've learnt from them and come to share their vision. It deals with any unhealthy sense of possessiveness. It's true that Paul wrote to the Corinthians from Ephesus reminding them, 'For in Christ Jesus I became your father through the gospel', but he preceded this by saying, 'You do not have many fathers.'[147] If he'd said, 'You have only one father, and I became your father through the gospel,' it would have sounded a very different note. In a church or project context, children can be seen as those who have had a new beginning through engaging with its vision. The takeaway from Psalm 127 is that they can achieve at least as much as their parents and will probably achieve more. I think this was something that Paul saw at Ephesus as those around him kept him from entering the arena during the riots as he prepared to leave. It was certainly something that I needed to see in moving forward.

So let me tell you how the repetition in 1 John 2:12-14 eventually made sense to me. You'll have noticed that to start with in these verses John addresses children (those young in their faith) and they get a double blessing. The words they receive as he runs through the list a second time are different from the original ones. Putting both together, they read, 'You know your sins have been forgiven on account of his name' and 'you know the Father'. That's great.

Coming to those who are a little more mature, their repetition covers the same ground concerning victory but then adds in more. Putting both together we have, 'You are strong, and the word of

---

147. 1 Corinthians 4:15.

14. Maturing: A necessary step forward

God lives in you, and you have overcome the evil one.' All of which sounds absolutely brilliant.

When it comes to fathers, who somehow end up sandwiched between children and young men, it's simply an exact repetition, as if God is keen to really hammer the point home, 'You know him who is from the beginning.' It doesn't actually say that you were around at the beginning, although that might have held true as at the time John was writing, the apostles did refer to the outpouring on the day of Pentecost as 'the beginning' and some might have actually been there (as John himself was). It's more likely that what is being implied is an intimate knowledge of God as Father, deep enough to understand and appreciate his heart as is evident in all he has done, not only since Pentecost but before the world was planned in eternity past, and, equally importantly, throughout their own lives as they journey with him. Well, put like that it really doesn't sound so bad. And there's more. Contrary to what I may first have thought, you don't lose what you had as you step up to the next level.

This is the really big revelation I'd been missing. I love interacting with everyone and it's great to know that I still have something in common with the children (forgiven sins and a relationship with the Father) and can still identify with the youths (in having strength, the indwelling word and a devil-overcoming mentality). Incredibly I can begin to see myself becoming more mature and having fellowship, not only with the One I've known from the beginning but with those I've looked up to from afar. The banding is not meant to restrict us, it's meant to liberate us. Much as I love those in my age group, life would lack so very, very much if relationships at that level were the only relationships considered appropriate for me to have. I've always been more than happy to reach across the years and it's great to know that I can grow up without losing out. I don't have to be a church-based equivalent of Peter Pan, the boy who never grew up.

Before I share with you the final point of this chapter, and indeed the whole book, let me share two stories, both a little gruesome (so apologies for that), which really inspire me. For the first we'll go back to Gideon and his pursuit that we talked about in chapters 5 and 9. We need to reach the point where his pursuit comes to an end. He's face to face with the kings of the Midianites.[148] They've not only devastated the land but have killed Gideon's brothers. The time has come to put an end to all the devastation and Gideon decides to give the honour of slaying the kings to his son. When his son baulks at it Zebah and Zalmunna, the Midianite kings, say to Gideon, 'Come, do it yourself. "As is the man, so is his strength."'[149] For me, in our prayer meetings when we were pursuing capital-wide problems, it would have been wonderful to have come that close to a breakthrough, and maybe we did. Gideon reminds me that battle honours can still go to the ones who've 'known him from the beginning'.

Two witnesses of course are better than one, and here is another story that encouraged me along the same lines. This one sounds even worse but it shows a side to Samuel that I never would have guessed existed. This time it isn't just the son of a champion like Gideon who's flunking his responsibilities but the King of Israel. Saul has been sent to bring God's judgement on some long-standing enemies with the commission to wipe out everyone and everything, bringing nothing back. But holding onto the livestock is too strong a temptation for Saul and he thinks he'll hold onto the local king for good measure. When Samuel visits Saul after the expedition, Saul is full of himself, having just set up a statue in his own honour, and boasts to Samuel

---

148. Judges 8:10-15.
149. Judges 8:18-21.

of carrying out God's instructions. To this Samuel replies with the memorable phrase, 'What then is this bleating of sheep in my ears?'[150] Knowing he has Saul on the back foot, he eventually asks him to bring out the king with whom Saul seems to have made some kind of truce, despite keeping him in chains. Samuel is having none of it and reminds the king, called Agag, of his bloodthirsty record. He then slays him on the spot.[151] With actions like that, who am I to think that strength goes when fatherhood is reached?

Coming to terms in this way with 1 John 2 may seem a far cry from the lessons I was learning from Psalms 127 and 23, but the illustrations I've used show Gideon and Samuel stepping in after they'd expected others to have matured sufficiently to carry out difficult assignments that at one time they might never have delegated. Their expectations were correct. As projects go forward they should gather their own momentum. People catch the vision and make progress. That progress will mean the children become youths and the youths become (in John's listing) 'fathers', but don't let's be unnecessarily gender specific. If I were to cling to 'youth' as being the highest level I wanted to aspire to, I could have aborted the very thing God had always wanted a teaching and training centre to be.

Let's pay a final visit to the School of Tyrannus and imagine there are people present from Smyrna, Pergamum, Thyatira, Sardis, Philadelphia, Laodicea, and perhaps even Colossus. How far would Paul have wanted them to develop under his teaching if they were to go out and establish churches, 'fathering people through the gospel'? I think the answer is clear. Our mandate likewise was not only to birth spiritual children and raise up spiritual youths, but to raise up

---

150. 1 Samuel 15:1-16.
151. 1 Samuel 15:32-33.

those who could go on and father others. Far from being Peter Pan, perhaps God was asking me to consider being a father to fathers. I was prepared to give it a go.

I realise that in this book I've tried to take you on Paul's journey as well as mine. There were enough similarities to make the fourteen steps I've shared a viable framework. I've tried to spare you nothing along the way and I hope you learn from what you may perceive to be my mistakes, just as you learn from what you can easily recognise as Paul's successes. I have not written to put you off from being a strategic vision-sharer and initiator, far from it. As much as possible, I've wanted to give you a practical handbook. I hope that I've managed to do that and that you have enjoyed the journey. My thoughts and prayers will be with you as you go forward.

Question:

How would you make sure you are not placing limits on anyone's development?

Postscript: *Strategic possibilities*

One of the reasons I started looking at Ephesus was the multiple windows of opportunity the New Testament provides for visiting that church over a period of some forty-five years.[152] Paul gave it his strategic attention for an intense period of two years, and may have had it in his sights for four years before that. In terms of follow-up, it's quite widely believed that Paul's first letter to Timothy implies a further visit by Paul to Ephesus after his release from house arrest in Rome. He was not anticipating such a visit when he said goodbye to the Ephesian elders at Miletus.[153] After Paul's death, John bases himself at Ephesus and Revelation shows what the church was like forty years after Paul had left.[154] It sounds as if the risen Jesus is saying it's time for a fresh strategic initiative, starting with a transformation of the church.

Whatever we achieved in the four or five years when we were trying to pick up London by its four corners, the reality is that the capital now needs something fresh. To be honest we didn't ever quite get to the point where we had four resource-centre churches working together from north, south, east and west to watch over London and intercede for it. The links we had with Kensington Temple and KICC were mainly through Mission to London. Somehow we were able to spur each other on while following different trajectories.

Kensington Temple was already well established and was an inspiration to us. It had a long-established reputation for hosting

---

152. Dating Paul's initial short visit as ad 42 and the book of Revelation as ad 97.
153. Acts 20:17-38. Referred to in chapter 10.
154. Revelation 2:1-7.

international speakers, sharing that honour at the time with a church in north London that we'd thought of engaging with but which seemed to be working through its own redevelopment plans. In Kensington Temple we were blessed with a lot of graciousness. We could have hit problems in setting up a central London Bible school as the International Bible Institute of London was a massive part of Kensington Temple's strategic thinking, but the church was so accommodating that we even shared lecturers. Interestingly, Kensington Temple was also well ahead of us in thinking about church planting and in looking at ways of maximising the training benefit of its congregation's midweek programme.

KICC, on the other hand, was growing fast and had a media interest. They were not far behind us in securing airtime on cable TV and were well ahead of us in taking programme slots on Christian radio. Even while we were working together on Mission to London (which Morris Cerullo did hand over to us, with Kensington Temple taking the lead), KICC was rapidly growing its own annual conference. Gathering of Champions soon became international and quickly proved to be a vital part of many people's spiritual journey and summer calendar.

So, what of strategic opportunities now? Well things are different. Maybe there are cities that can be picked up by their corners, but they are more likely to be picked up community by community, which in many ways makes more sense. There are many churches emerging with younger leadership that are attracting younger congregations. Many of these have a worship and word emphasis that could well lead into the kind of watchful intercessory role that we felt led to engage with. Given my background in interchurch relations, it won't come as a surprise that I think the impact of such engagement would be greater if there were more initiatives encouraging everyone to work together. I'm delighted, though, that such initiatives are beginning to happen again, and generally I believe that London is in a better place church-wise. There are definitely many more dynamic churches in London now than there were, and, despite central London traffic challenges, we once again have some strong churches in the centre.

Many churches across the capital are working to some kind of strategic mission statement and all of this is progress. Media links are stronger than they were, and if we do manage to promote more targeted prayer, the issues that we dealt with would probably not be the ones I would focus on today, and that's a good sign. Things move on and prayer plays a part in making that happen. I still meet with some of London's senior church leaders and a lot of gracious listening takes place. This is a good start, but we know there are issues to grapple with, although it's tempting to prefer the safety of common ground. Let's all pray for (and with) greater boldness.

But the message of this book is not limited to London. Globally, opportunities for strategically-shaped churches and strategically-driven projects are endless. My hope is that this book will have inspired you to find a God-given goal and to work unstintingly towards it, perhaps drawing on Paul's experience in Ephesus along the way. If, at the same time, you have found that looking at our experience in south-east London has been helpful, it will be God who deserves the credit. Personally, I'm only too aware of the limitations and areas of inefficiency demonstrated in this particular phase of our ongoing attempt to be strategic. I hope that my honesty has helped, and that you can see that we actually learnt some things in the process. If it's God's faithfulness in the face of our limitations that has inspired you, my prayer is that that will always be the case.

www.ingramcontent.com/pod-product-compliance
Lightning Source LLC
Chambersburg PA
CBHW070156100426
42743CB00013B/2927